2nd Edition

PIANO • VOCAL • GUITAR

# more of THE BEST STANDARDS EVER

## VOLUME 2 (M-Z)

ISBN 978-0-634-03747-4

# HAL•LEONARD®
## CORPORATION

7777 W. BLUEMOUND RD. P.O. BOX 13819 MILWAUKEE, WI 53213

Visit Hal Leonard Online at
**www.halleonard.com**

# CONTENTS

*more of* **THE BEST STANDARDS EVER – Vol. 2**

# MAKE SOMEONE HAPPY

**from DO RE MI**

Words by BETTY COMDEN and ADOLPH GREEN
Music by JULE STYNE

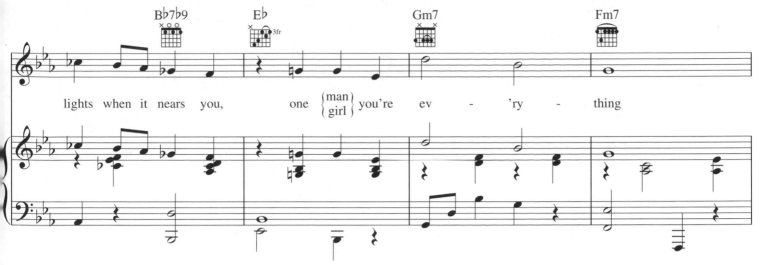

lights when it nears you, one {man/girl} you're ev - 'ry - thing

to. Fame, _____ if you win it, comes and goes _

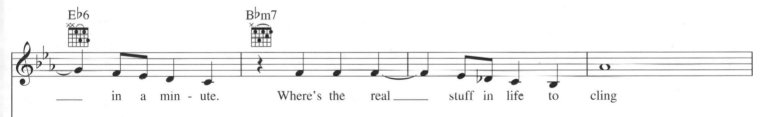

_____ in a min - ute. Where's the real ____ stuff in life to cling

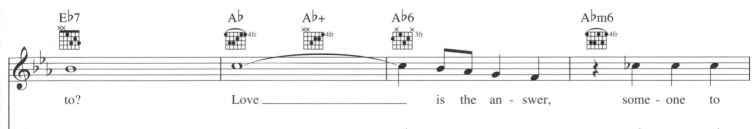

to? Love _____ is the an - swer, some - one to

love is the an - swer. Once you've found (him,) (her,)

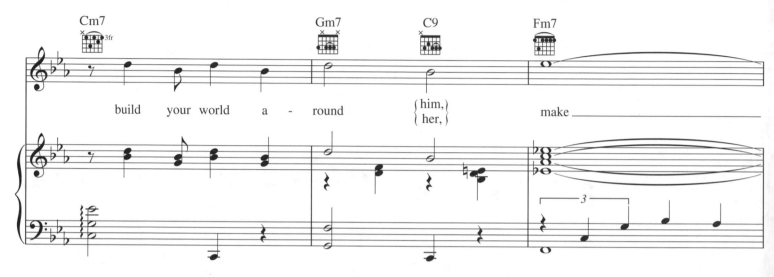

build your world a - round (him,) (her,) make _____

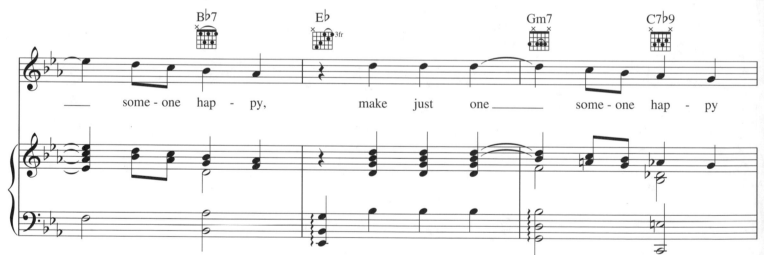

_____ some - one hap - py, make just one _____ some - one hap - py

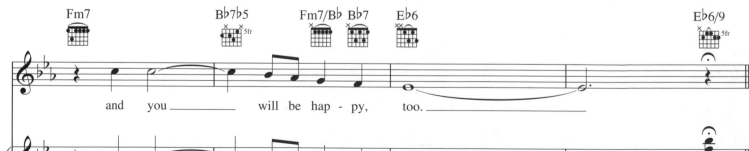

and you _____ will be hap - py, too. _____

# MIDNIGHT SUN

Words and Music by LIONEL HAMPTON,
SONNY BURKE and JOHNNY MERCER

af - ter you were gone, there was still some star - dust on my sleeve.

The flame of it may dwin - dle to an em - ber, and the stars for -

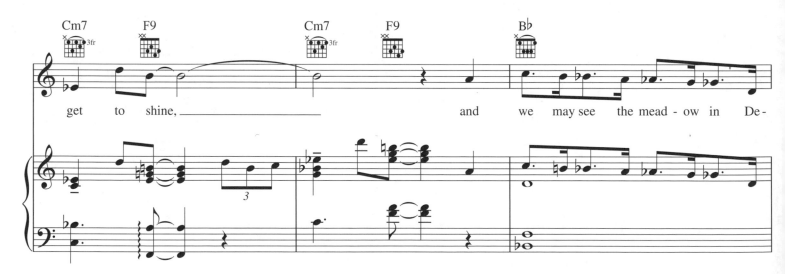

get to shine, and we may see the mead - ow in De -

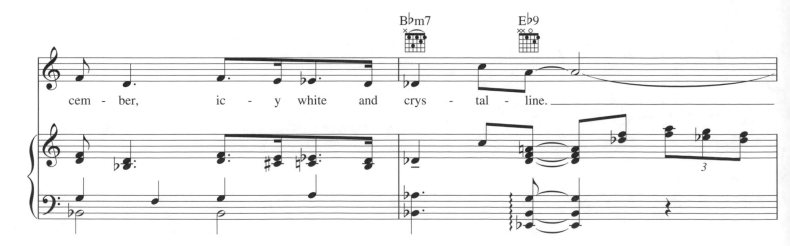

cem - ber, ic - y white and crys - tal - line.

But, oh, my dar - ling, al - ways I'll re -

mem - ber when your lips were close to mine

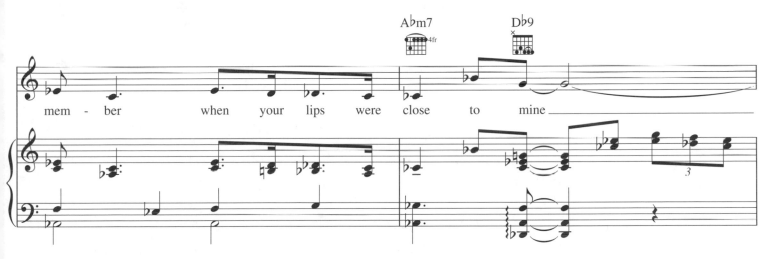

and { I } { we } saw the mid - night sun.

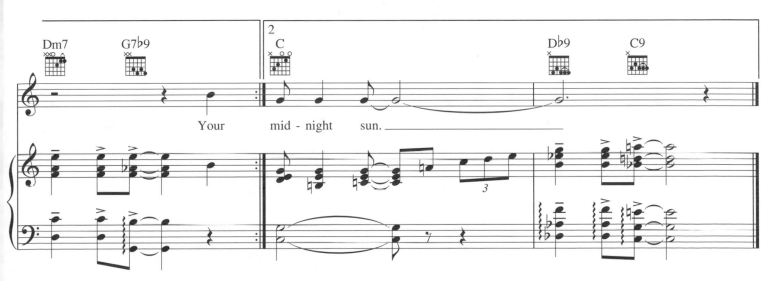

Your mid - night sun.

# MAKIN' WHOOPEE!
## from WHOOPEE!

Lyrics by GUS KAHN
Music by WALTER DONALDSON

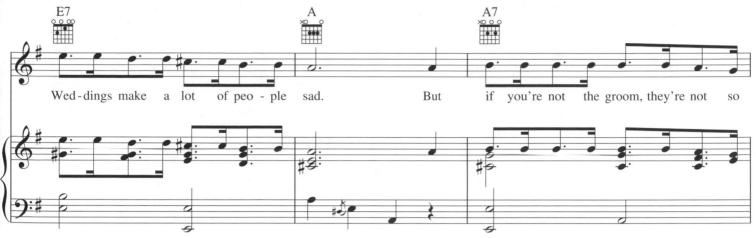

Wed-dings make a lot of peo-ple sad. But if you're not the groom, they're not so

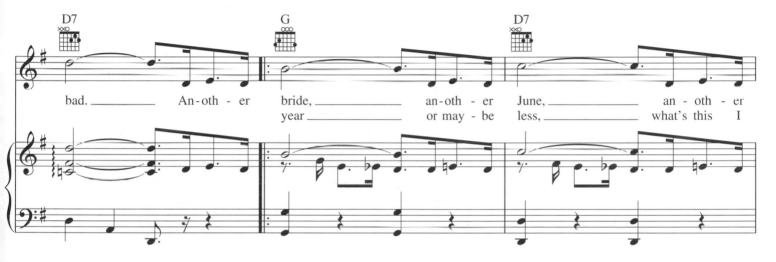

bad. _____ An-oth-er bride, _____ an-oth-er June, _____ an-oth-er
year _____ or may-be less, _____ what's this I

sun - ny hon-ey - moon. _____ An-oth-er sea - son, _____ an-oth-er
hear? _____ Well, can't you guess? _____ She feels ne-glect - ed, _____ and he's sus-

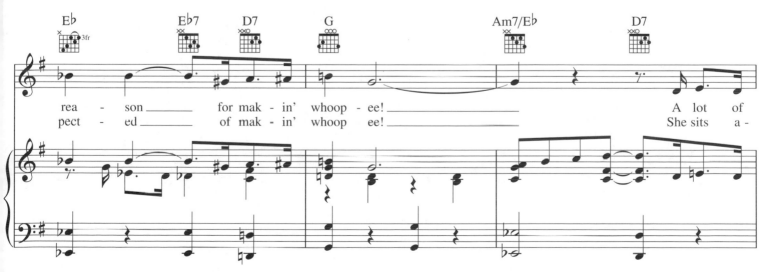

rea - son _____ for mak-in' whoop-ee! _____ A lot of
pect - ed _____ of mak-in' whoop ee! _____ She sits a-

shoes, _____ a lot of rice, _____ the groom is nerv - ous, _____ he an - swers
lone _____ 'most ev - 'ry night, _____ he does - n't 'phone her, _____ he does - n't

twice. _____ It's real - ly kill - ing _____ that he's so will - ing _____ to make
write. _____ He says he's "bus - y," _____ but she says "is he?" _____ He's mak - in'

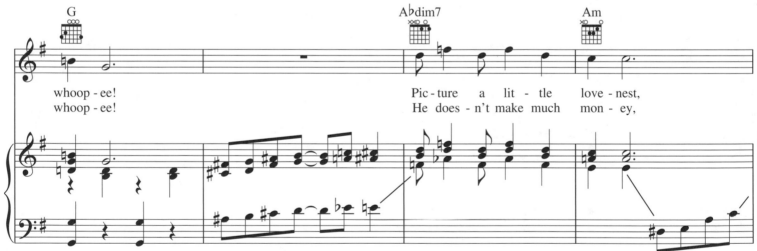

whoop - ee!
whoop - ee!       Pic - ture a lit - tle love - nest,
He does - n't make much mon - ey,

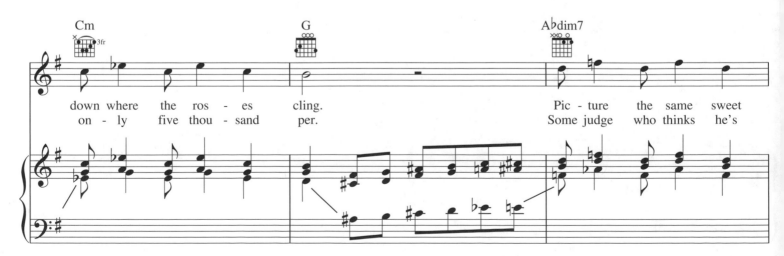

down where the ros - es cling.       Pic - ture the same sweet
on - ly five thou - sand per.       Some judge who thinks he's

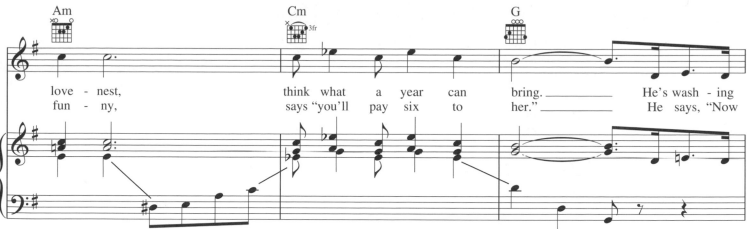

love - nest,  think what  a  year  can  bring._____  He's wash - ing
fun - ny,  says "you'll  pay  six  to  her."_____  He says, "Now

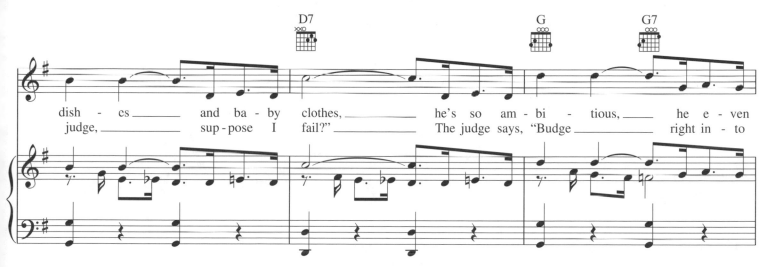

dish - es_____  and ba - by  clothes,_____  he's so am - bi - tious,_____  he e - ven
judge,_____  sup - pose I  fail?"_____  The judge says, "Budge_____  right in - to

sews._____  But don't for - get,  folks,_____  that's what you  get,  folks,_____  for mak - in'
jail._____  You'd bet - ter keep  her,_____  I think it's cheap - er_____  than mak - in'

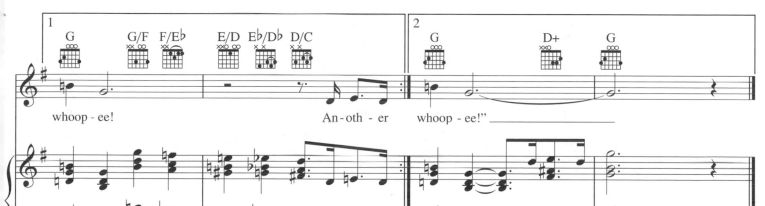

whoop - ee!  An - oth - er  whoop - ee!"_____

# MONA LISA

### from the Paramount Picture CAPTAIN CAREY, U.S.A.

Words and Music by JAY LIVINGSTON
and RAY EVANS

Li - sa, Mo - na Li - sa, men have named you. You're so

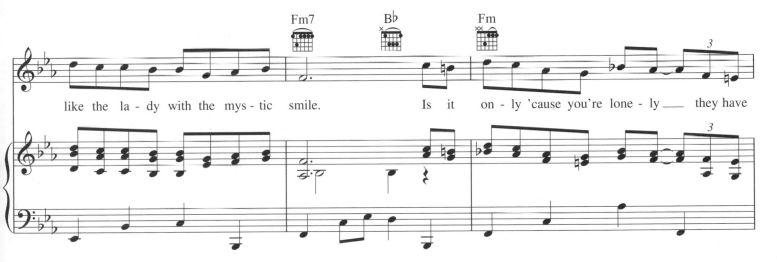

like the la - dy with the mys - tic smile. Is it on - ly 'cause you're lone - ly ___ they have

blamed you for that Mo - na Li - sa strange - ness ___ in your smile? Do you

smile to tempt a lov - er, ___ Mo - na Li - sa, ___ or is

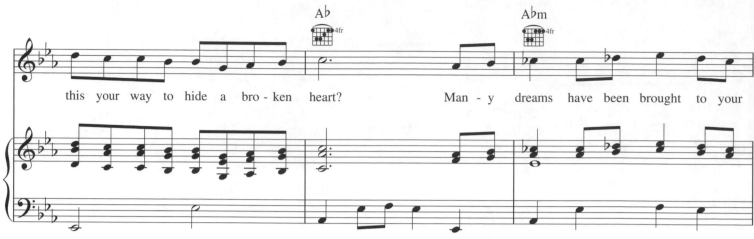

this your way to hide a bro-ken heart? Man-y dreams have been brought to your

door-step. They just lie there, and they die there. Are you

warm, are you real, Mo - na Li - sa, or just a

cold and lone-ly, love-ly work of art? Mo - na art?

# MOON RIVER

from the Paramount Picture BREAKFAST AT TIFFANY'S

Words by JOHNNY MERCER
Music by HENRY MANCINI

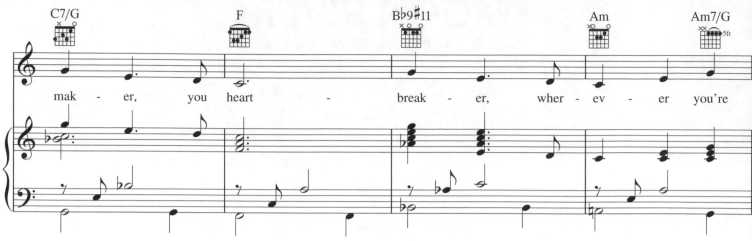

mak - er, you heart - break - er, wher - ev - er you're

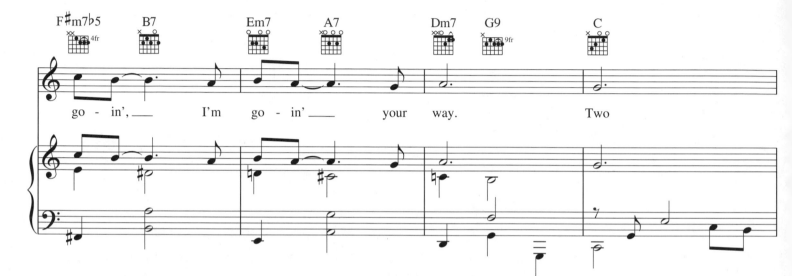

go - in', \_\_\_ I'm go - in' \_\_\_ your way. Two

drift - ers, off to see the world. There's such a lot of

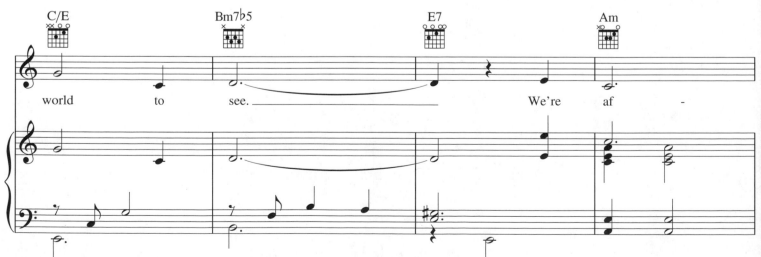

world to see. _____ We're af -

# MOOD INDIGO
## from SOPHISTICATED LADIES

Words and Music by DUKE ELLINGTON,
IRVING MILLS and ALBANY BIGARD

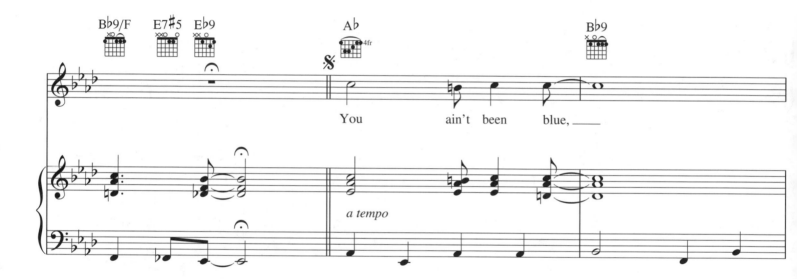

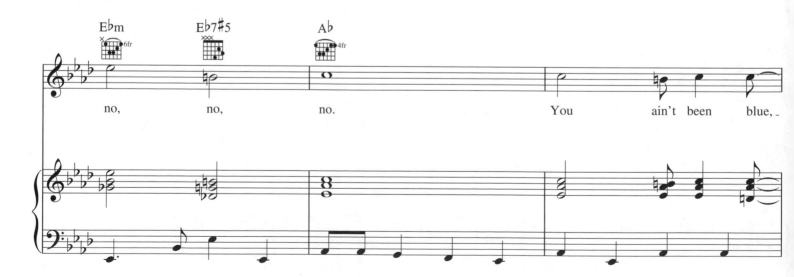

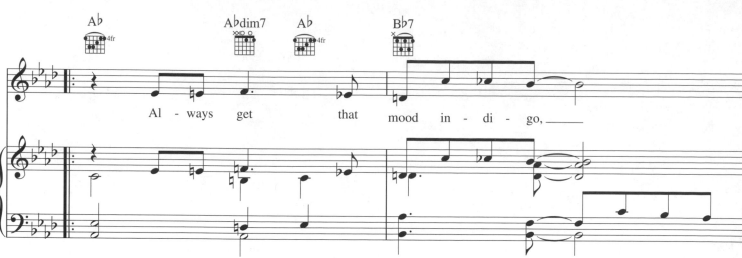

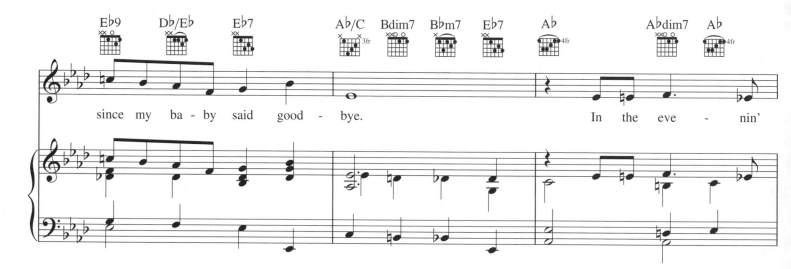

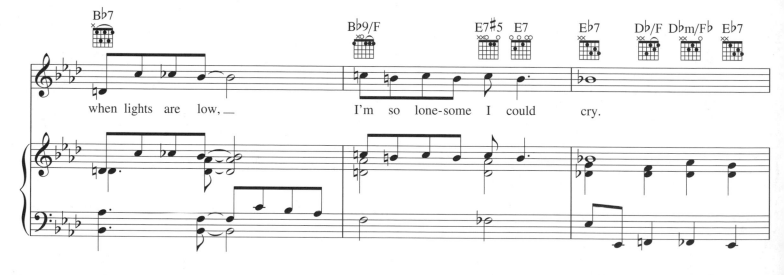

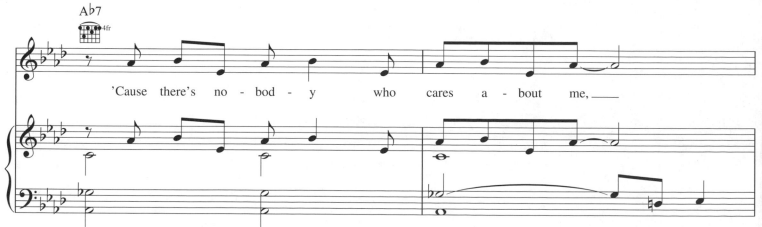

I'm just a soul who's blu-er than blue ___ can be.

When I get that mood in-di-go, ___

I could lay me down and die.

die.

"Go 'long blues."

# MOONGLOW

Words and Music by WILL HUDSON,
EDDIE DE LANGE and IRVING MILLS

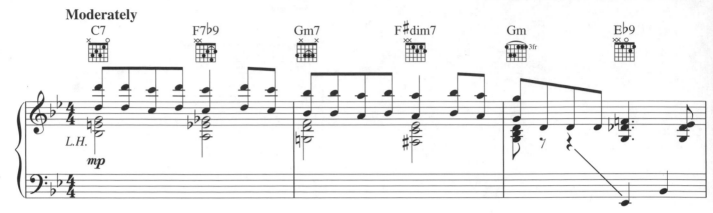

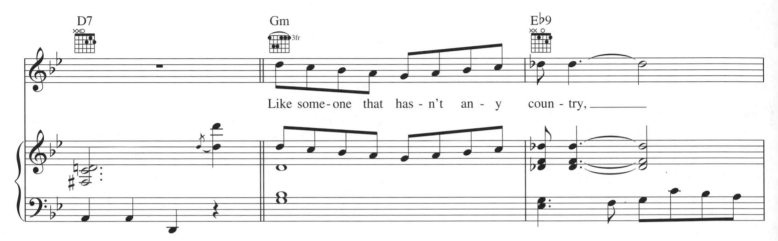

Like some-one that has-n't an-y coun-try, _____

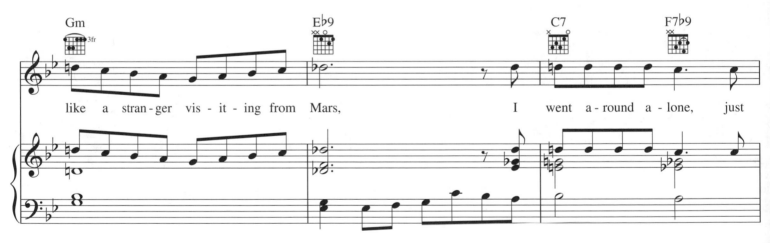

like a stran-ger vis-it-ing from Mars, I went a-round a-lone, just

like a roll-ing stone un-til I read a mes-sage in the stars:

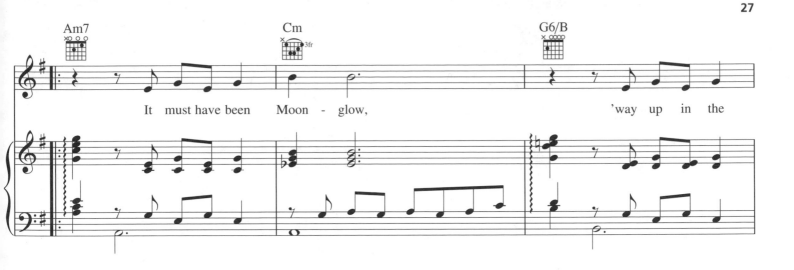

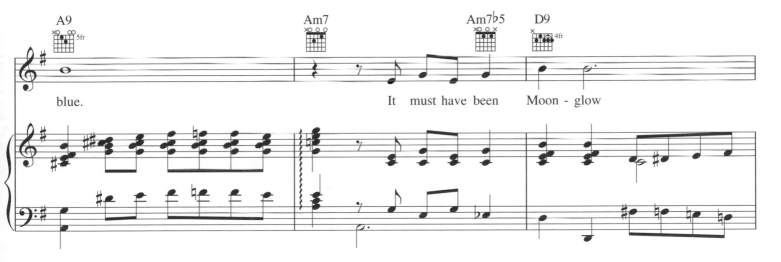

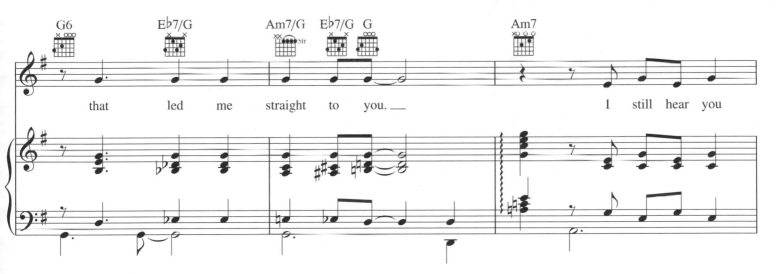

And I start in pray-ing, Oh Lord, please

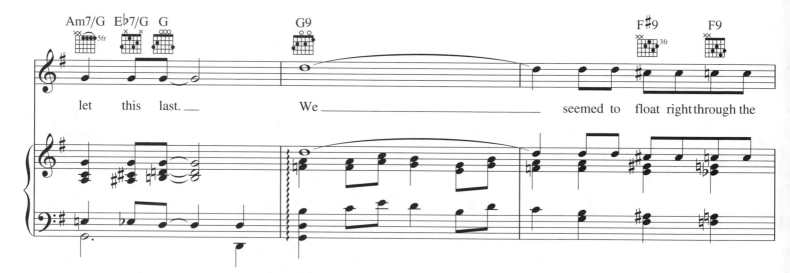

let this last. __ We __ seemed to float right through the

air. __ Heav-en-ly songs __

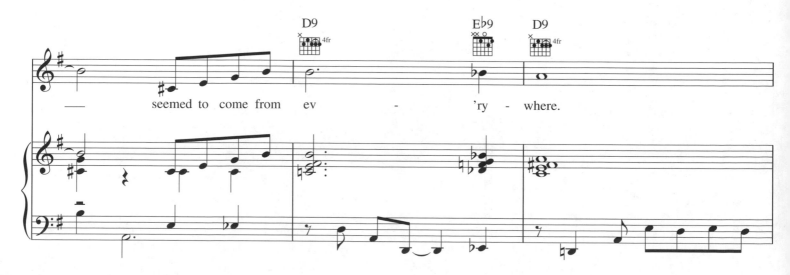

__ seemed to come from ev- - 'ry - where.

# MOONLIGHT IN VERMONT

Words and Music by JOHN BLACKBURN
and KARL SUESSDORF

ski trails on a moun-tain-side, snow-light in Ver-

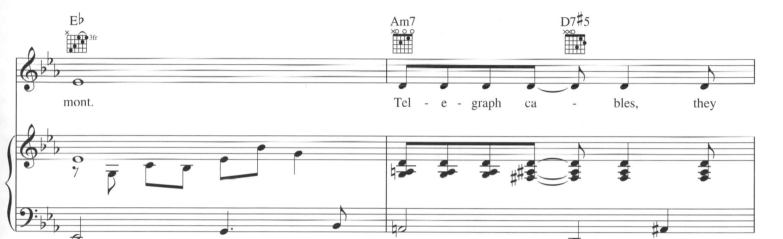

mont. Tel - e - graph ca - bles, they

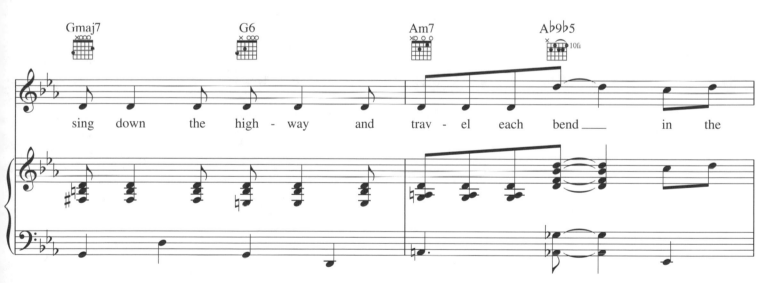

sing down the high - way and trav - el each bend ___ in the

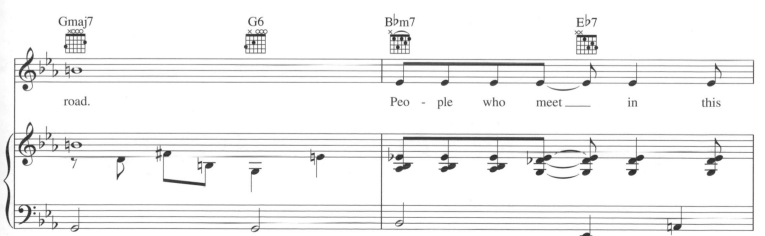

road. Peo - ple who meet ___ in this

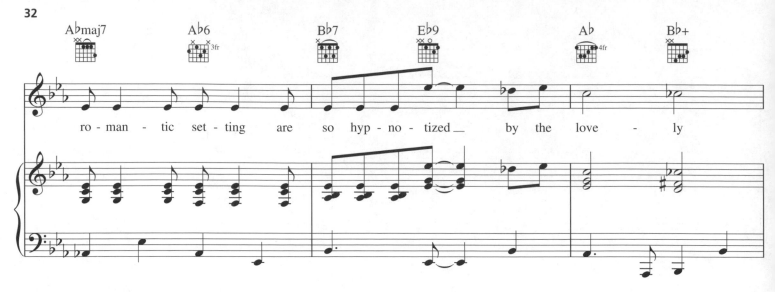

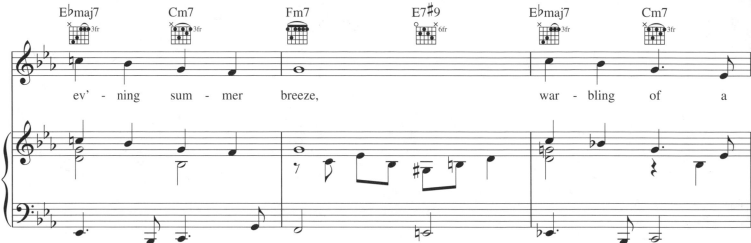

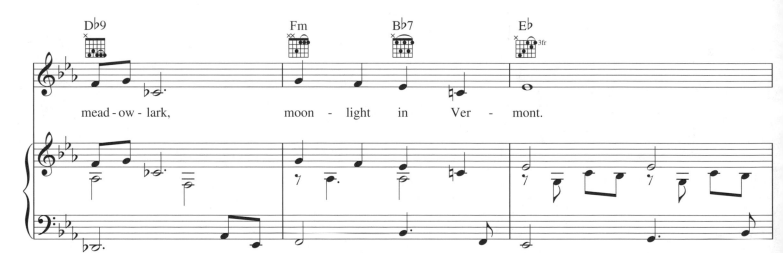

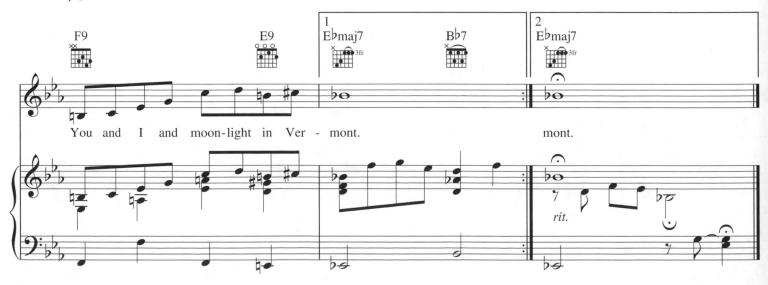

# MY BLUE HEAVEN

Lyric by GEORGE WHITING
Music by WALTER DONALDSON

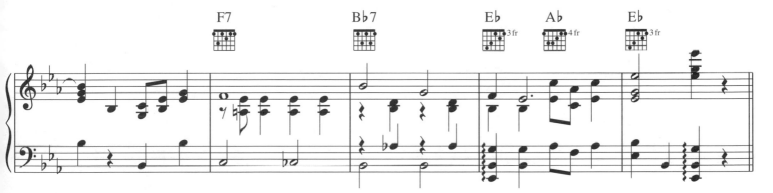

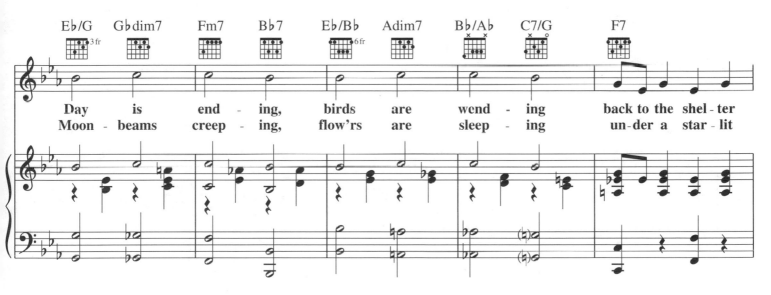

Day     is     end - ing,     birds     are     wend - ing     back to the shel - ter
Moon - beams     creep - ing,     flow'rs     are     sleep - ing     un - der a star - lit

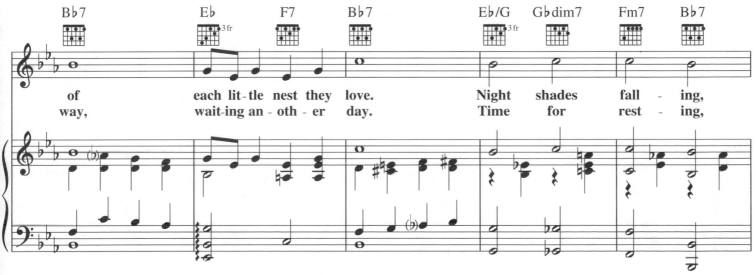

of          each lit - tle nest they love.          Night     shades          fall - ing,
way,        wait - ing an - oth - er   day.          Time     for          rest - ing,

# MORE
## (Ti guarderò nel cuore)
### from the Film MONDO CANE

Music by NINO OLIVIERO and RIZ ORTOLANI
Italian Lyrics by MARCELLO CIORCIOLINI
English Lyrics by NORMAN NEWELL

Moderately

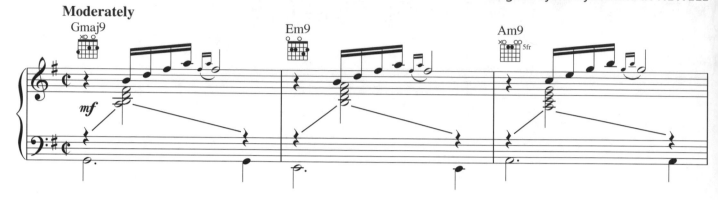

More
Se

than the great-est love the
tu mi guar- di in fon- do al

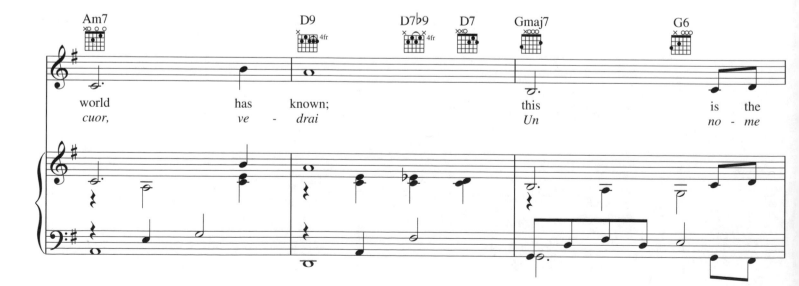

world
cuor,

has known;
ve - drai

this
Un

is the
no - me

# MY FAVORITE THINGS
## from THE SOUND OF MUSIC

Lyrics by OSCAR HAMMERSTEIN II
Music by RICHARD RODGERS

# MY FOOLISH HEART

from MY FOOLISH HEART

Words by NED WASHINGTON
Music by VICTOR YOUNG

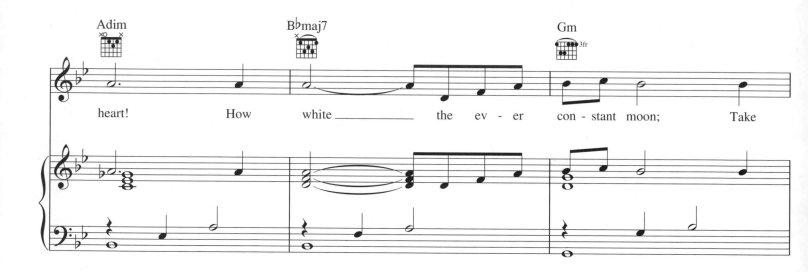

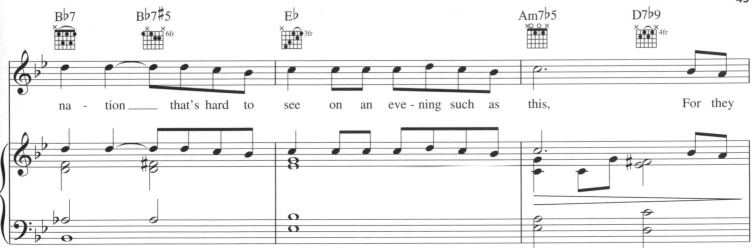

na - tion _____ that's hard to see on an eve - ning such as this, For they

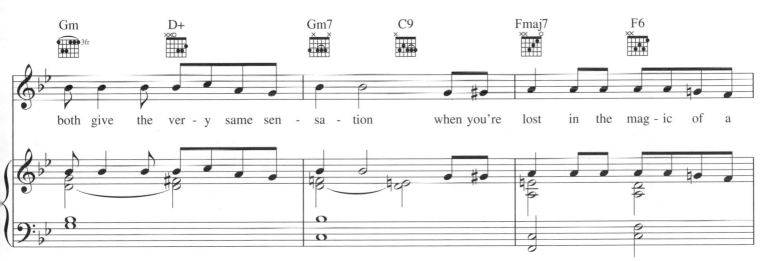

both give the ver - y same sen - sa - tion when you're lost in the mag - ic of a

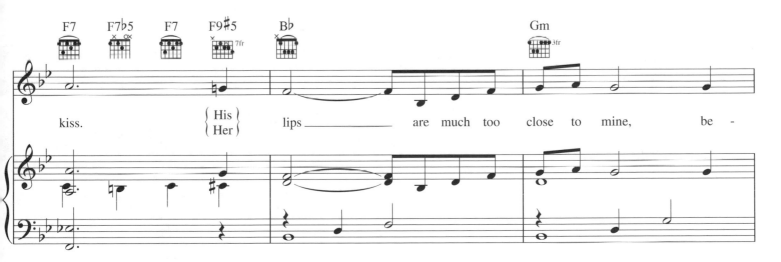

kiss. His/Her lips _____ are much too close to mine, be -

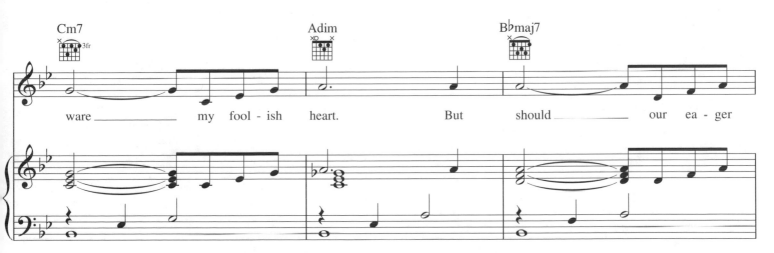

ware _____ my fool - ish heart. But should _____ our ea - ger

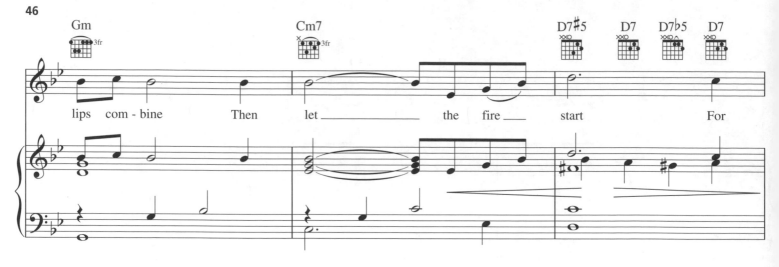

lips com-bine Then let _____ the fire ____ start For

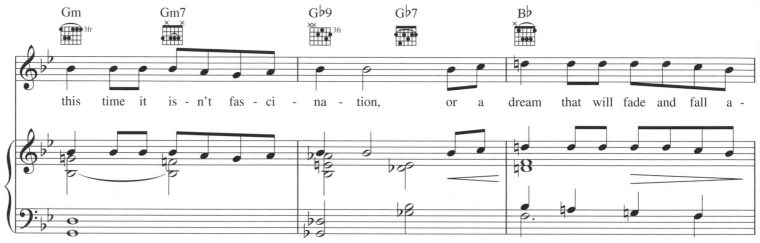

this time it is-n't fas-ci-na-tion, or a dream that will fade and fall a-

part, It's love _____ this time, it's love, my fool-ish

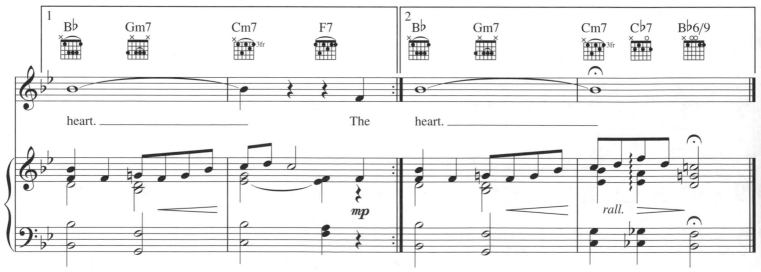

heart. _____ The heart. _____

# MY IDEAL

from the Paramount Picture PLAYBOY OF PARIS

Words by LEO ROBIN
Music by RICHARD A. WHITING and NEWELL CHASE

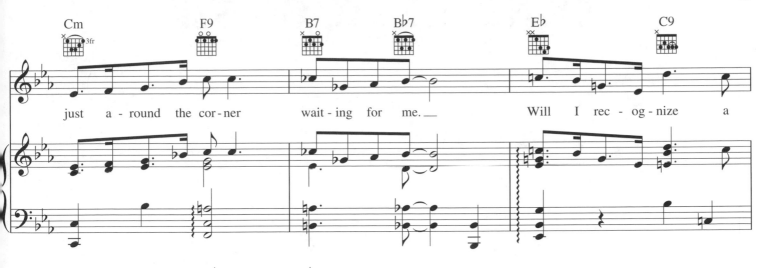

just a-round the cor-ner wait-ing for me. __ Will I rec-og-nize a

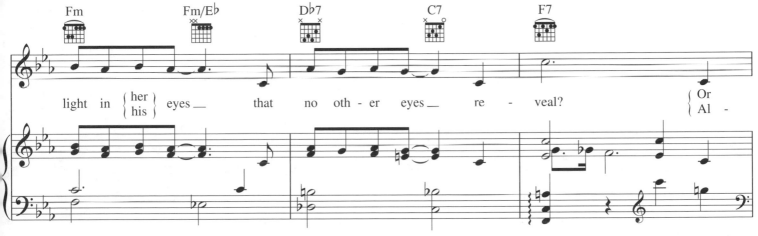

light in {her / his} eyes __ that no oth-er eyes __ re - veal? {Or / Al -}

will I pass {him / her} by and nev-er e-ven know that {he / she} is my i -

though {she / he} may be late, I trust in fate and so I wait for my i -

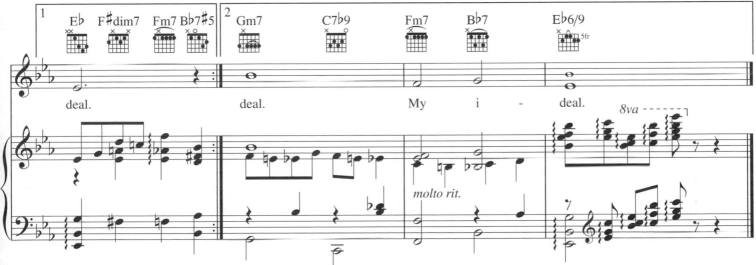

deal.     deal.    My i - deal.

# MY HEART STOOD STILL
## from A CONNECTICUT YANKEE

Words by LORENZ HART
Music by RICHARD RODGERS

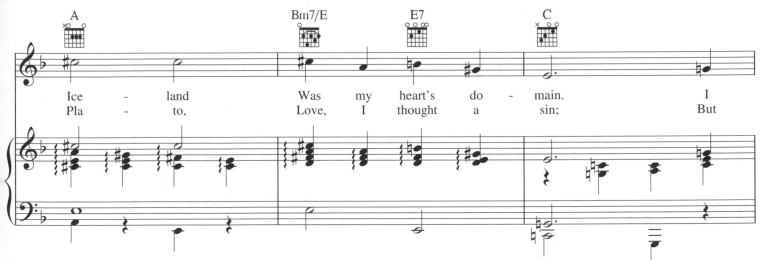

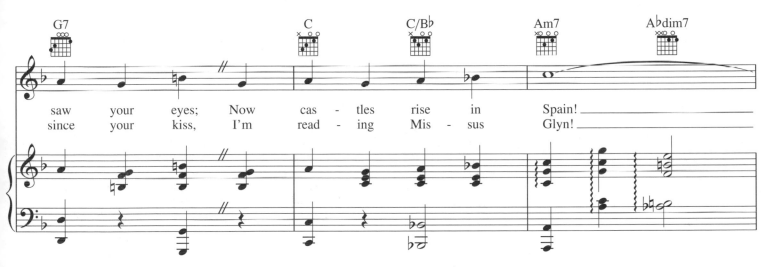

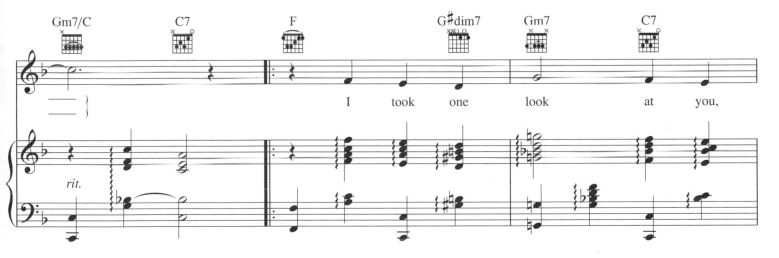

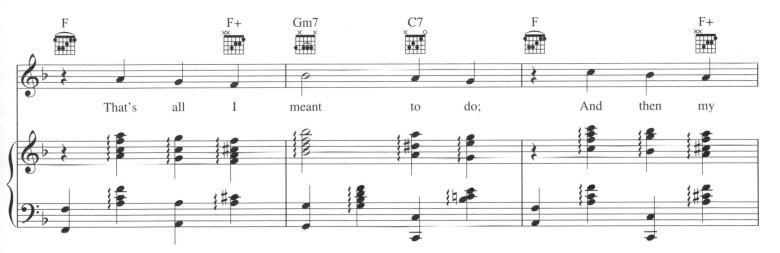

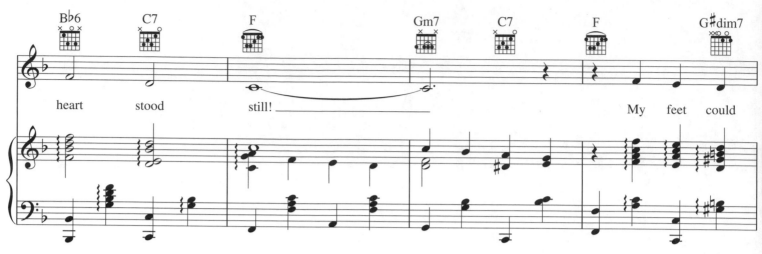

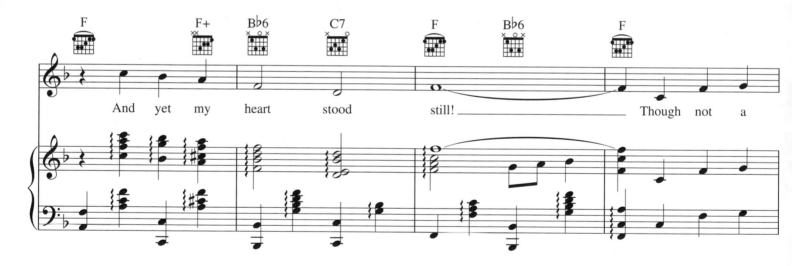

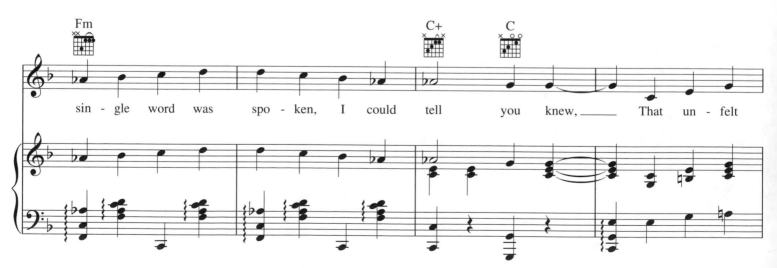

clasp of hands _____ Told me so well you knew. _____

I nev - er lived at all Un - til the

thrill of that mo - ment when My heart stood

still. still. _____

# MY OLD FLAME

## from the Paramount Picture BELLE OF THE NINETIES

Words and Music by ARTHUR JOHNSTON
and SAM COSLOW

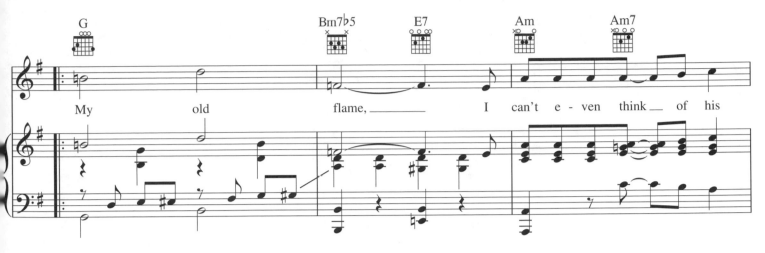

My old flame, ___ I can't e - ven think ___ of his

name but it's fun - ny now and then how my thoughts go flash - ing back a - gain ___ to

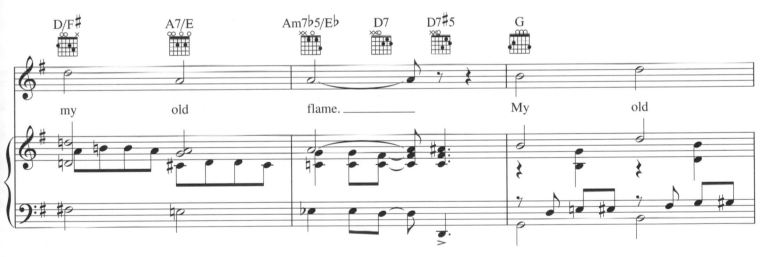

my old flame. ___ My old

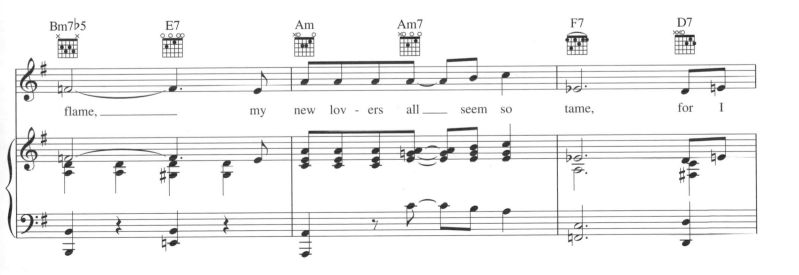

flame, ___ my new lov - ers all ___ seem so tame, for I

have-n't met a gent so mag - nif - i - cent or el - e - gant__ as my old

flame._____ I've met so man - y who had fas - ci - nat - in' ways,__ a

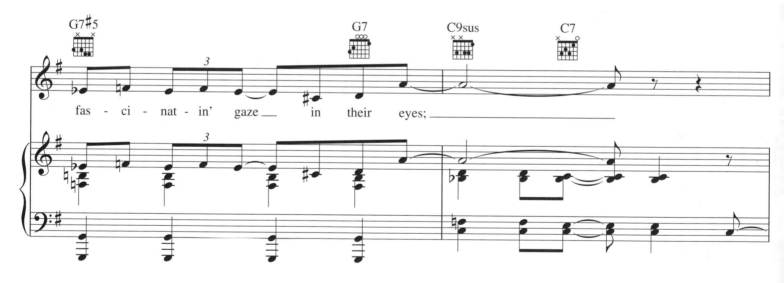

fas - ci - nat - in' gaze__ in their eyes;_____

some who took me up__ to the skies._____ But

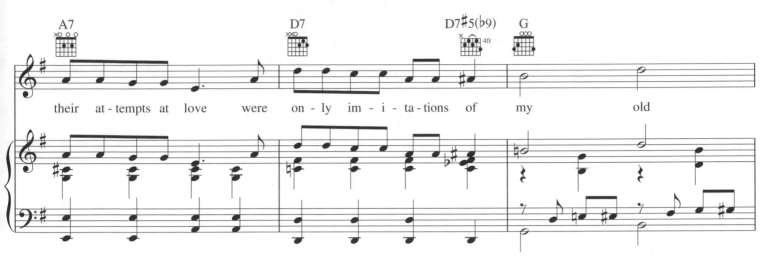

their at-tempts at love were on-ly im-i-ta-tions of my old

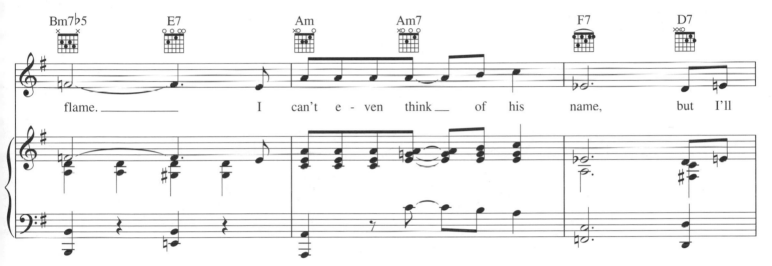

flame. _____ I can't e-ven think __ of his name, but I'll

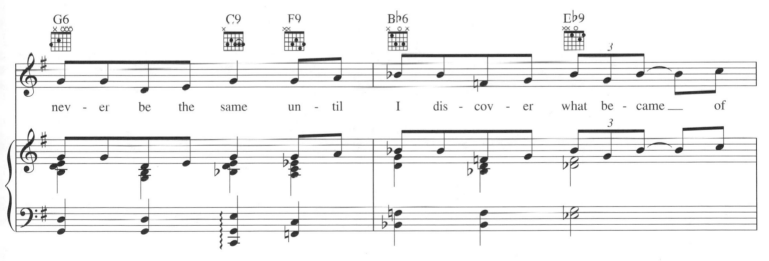

nev-er be the same un-til I dis-cov-er what be-came __ of

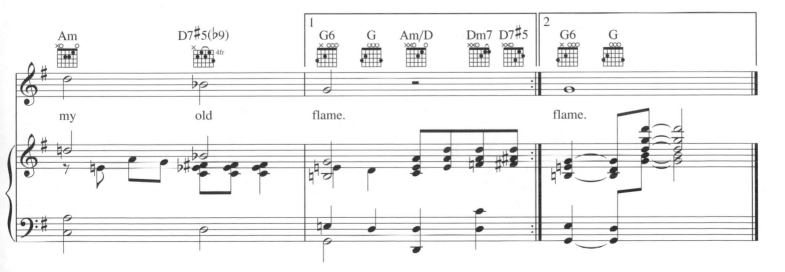

my old flame. flame.

# MY SHIP
## from the Musical Production LADY IN THE DARK

Words by IRA GERSHWIN
Music by KURT WEILL

Moderately slow

Lyrics:
My ship has sails that are made of silk. The decks are trimmed with gold. And of jam and spice there's a par-a-dise in the hold. _____

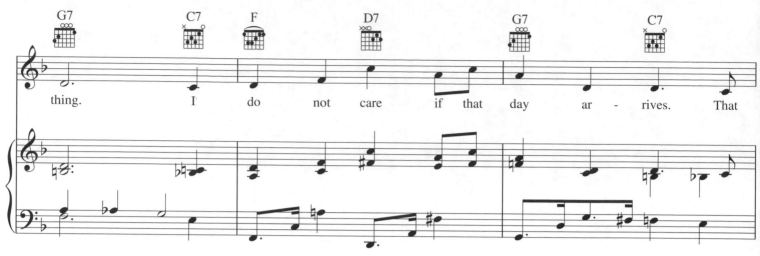

thing. I do not care if that day ar - rives. That

dream need nev - er be, if the ship I sing does-n't al - so bring my

**Slower**

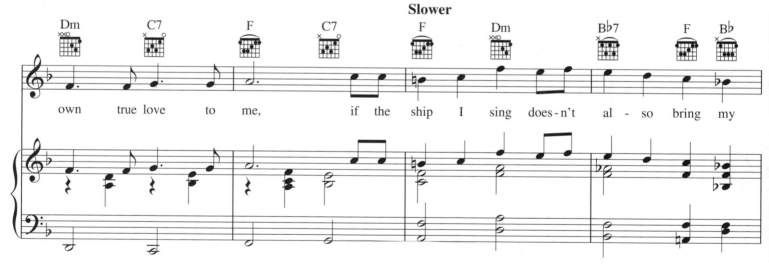

own true love to me, if the ship I sing does-n't al - so bring my

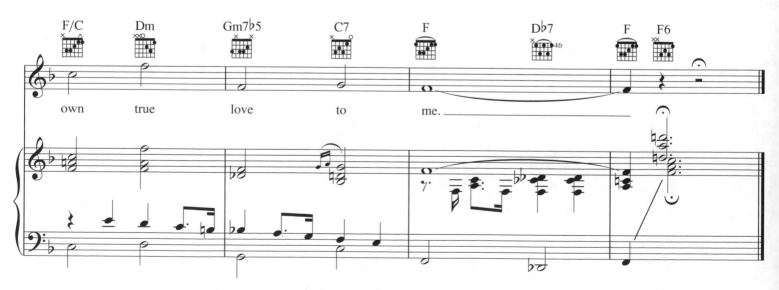

own true love to me. \_\_\_\_\_

# NATURE BOY

Words and Music by
EDEN AHBEZ

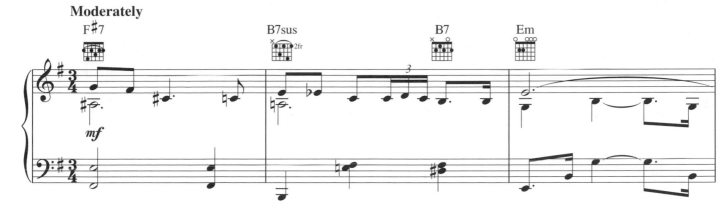

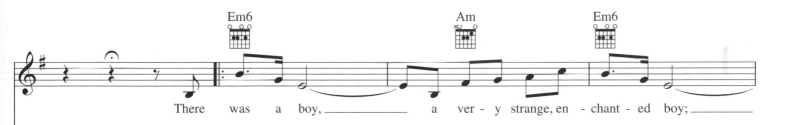

There was a boy, _____ a ver - y strange, en - chant - ed boy; _____

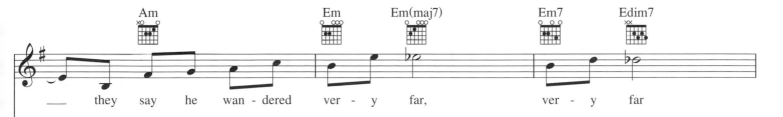

____ they say he wan - dered ver - y far, ver - y far

o - ver land and sea. A lit - tle shy _____ and

sad of eye, _____ but ver - y wise _____ was

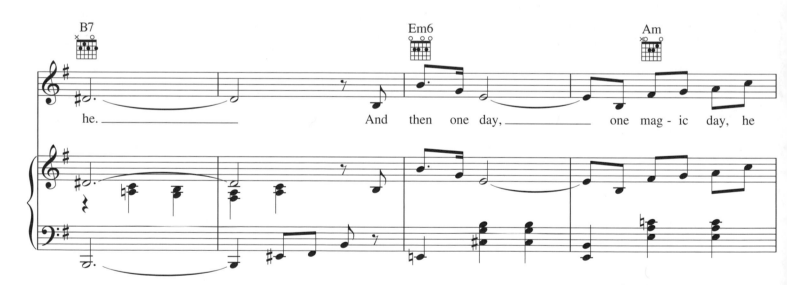

he. _____ And then one day, _____ one mag - ic day, he

passed my way and as we spoke of man - y things,

fools and kings, this he said to me: "The

great - est thing _____ you'll ev - er learn _____ is

just to love and be loved _ in re - turn." There

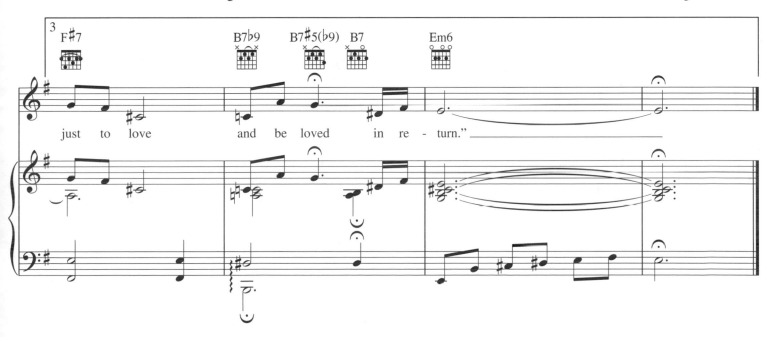

just to love and be loved in re - turn." _____

# MY SILENT LOVE

Words by EDWARD HEYMAN
Music by DANA SUESSE

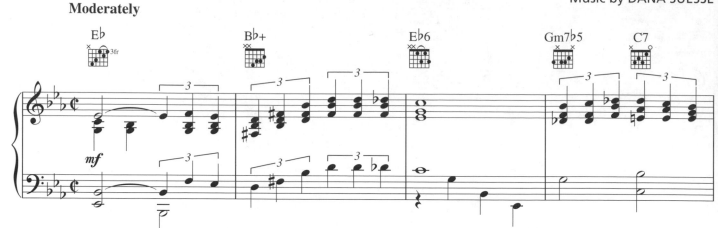

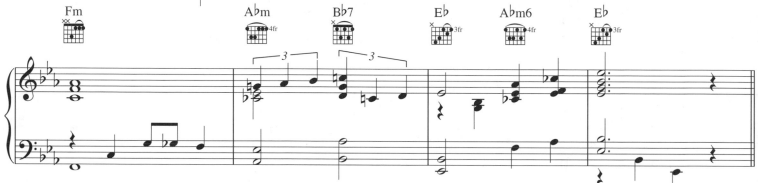

You would on-ly spurn my love if I had shown it.

You would sure-ly turn my love a-way.

# THE NEARNESS OF YOU

### from the Paramount Picture ROMANCE IN THE DARK

Words by NED WASHINGTON
Music by HOAGY CARMICHAEL

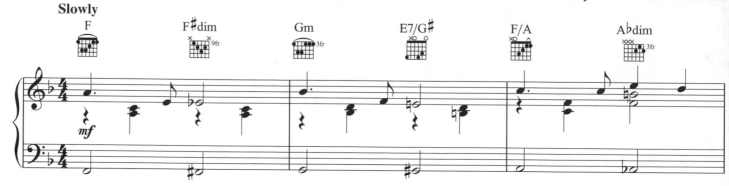

Why do I just with-er and for-get all re-sist-ance when

you and your mag-ic pass by? My heart's in a dith-er, dear, when

you're at a dis-tance, but when you are near, oh my! _____ It's not the

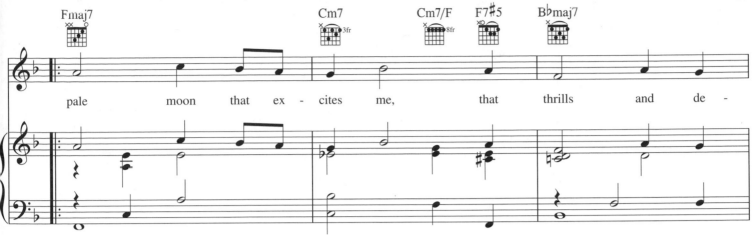

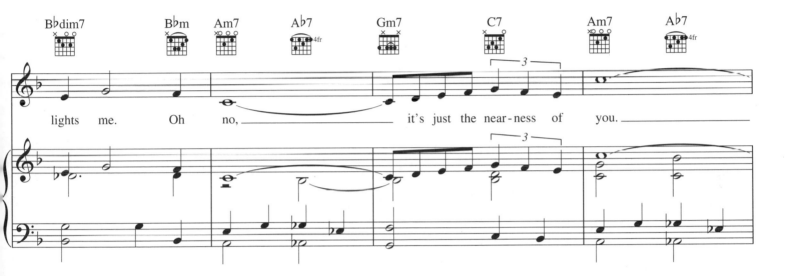

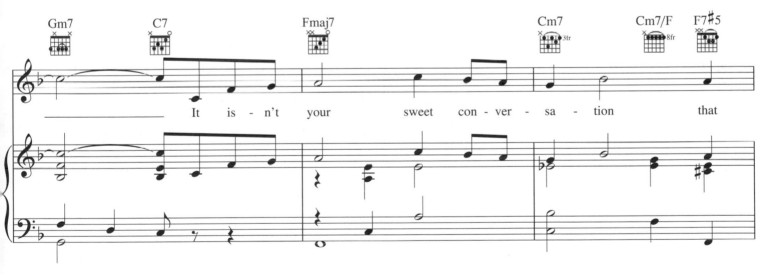

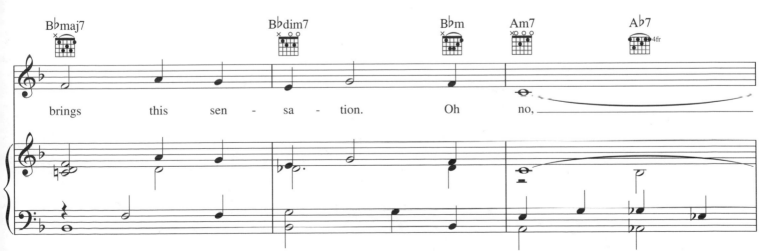

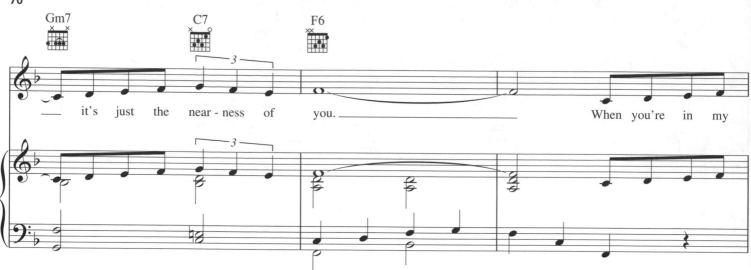

it's just the near-ness of you. When you're in my

arms and I feel you so close to me, all my

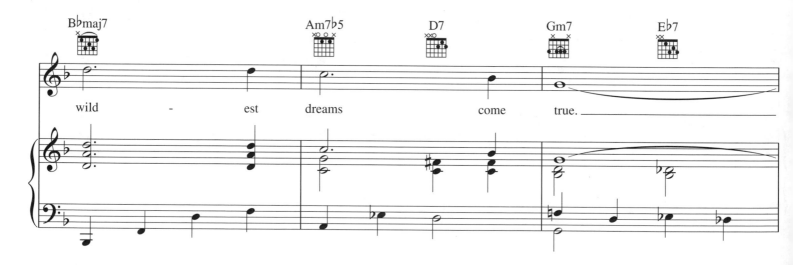

wild - est dreams come true.

I need no soft lights to en-chant me if

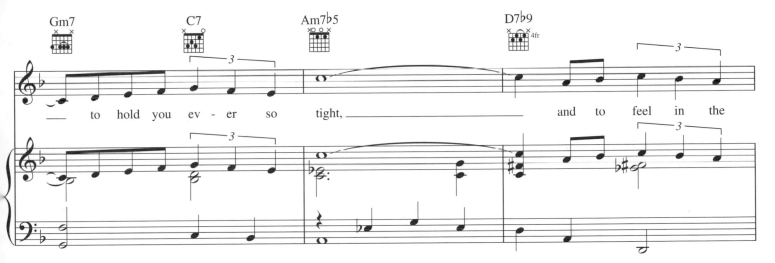

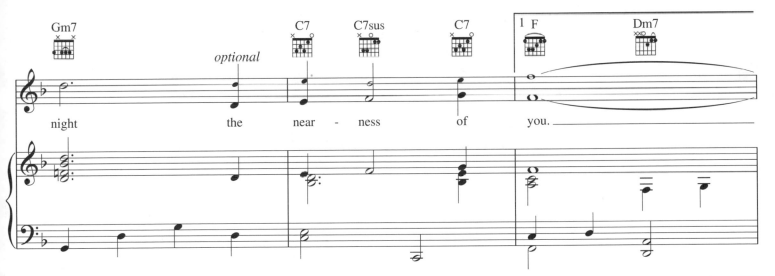

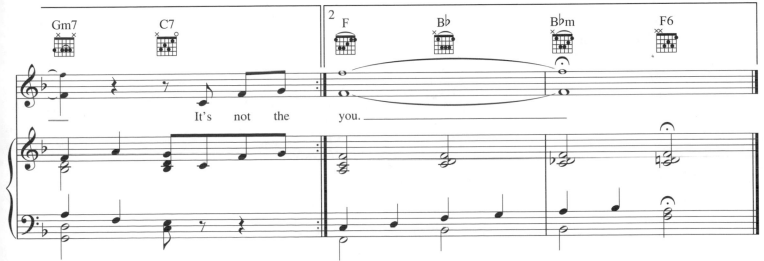

# NEVER LET ME GO
## from the Paramount Picture THE SCARLET HOUR

Words and Music by JAY LIVINGSTON
and RAY EVANS

**Slowly and poignantly, with a quiet beat**

# A NIGHTINGALE SANG IN BERKELEY SQUARE

Lyric by ERIC MASCHWITZ
Music by MANNING SHERWIN

When true lov-ers meet in May-fair, so the leg-ends tell, song-birds sing, win-ter turns to spring, ev-'ry wind-ing street in May-fair falls be-neath the spell. I

know such en - chant - ment can be, 'cause it hap - pened one eve - ning to

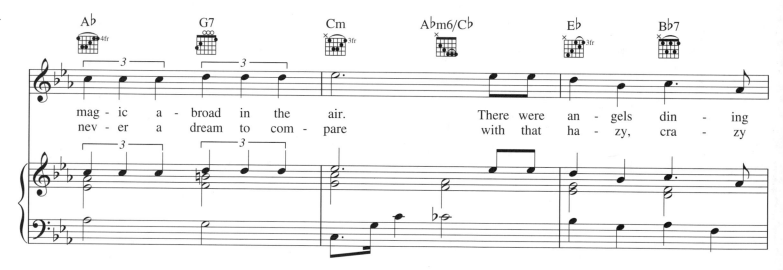

me. That cer - tain night, the night we met, there was

strange it was, how sweet and strange. There was

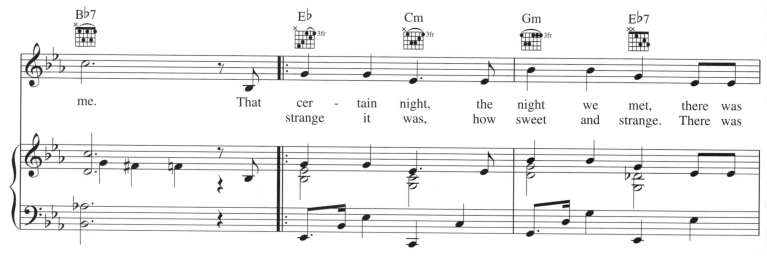

mag - ic a - broad in the air. There were an - gels din - ing

nev - er a dream to com - pare with that ha - zy, cra - zy

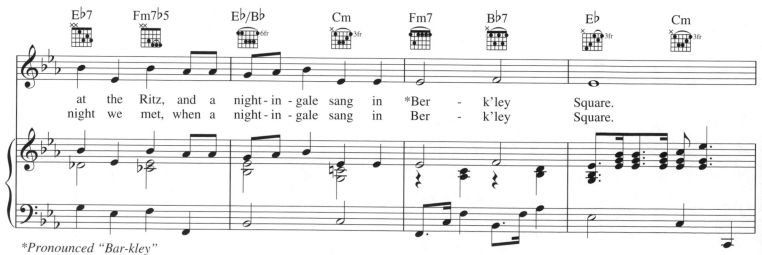

at the Ritz, and a night - in - gale sang in *Ber - k'ley Square.

night we met, when a night - in - gale sang in Ber - k'ley Square.

*Pronounced "Bar-kley"

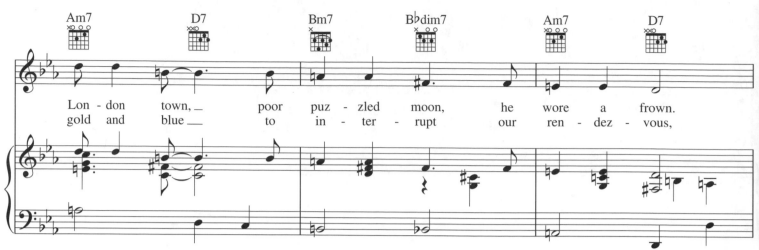

Lon - don town, __ poor puz - zled moon, he wore a frown.
gold and blue __ to in - ter - rupt our ren - dez - vous,

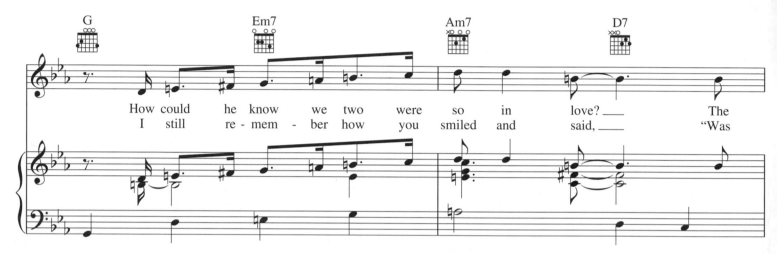

How could he know we two were so in love? __ The
I still re - mem - ber how were you smiled and said, __ "Was

whole darn world seemed up - side down. The streets of town were
that a dream seemed or was it down. Our home - ward step was

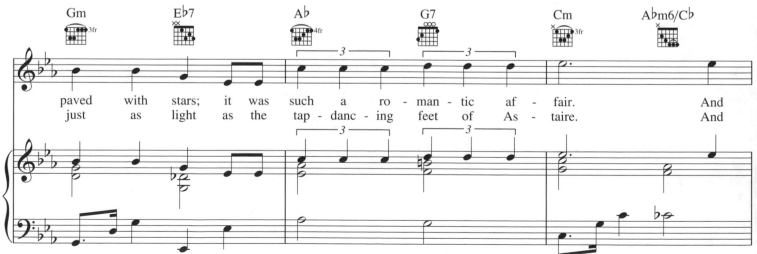

paved with stars; it was such a ro - man - tic af - fair. And
just as light as the tap - danc - ing feet of As - taire. And

as we kissed and said "good-night," a night-in-gale sang in
like an ech - o far a - way, a night-in-gale sang in

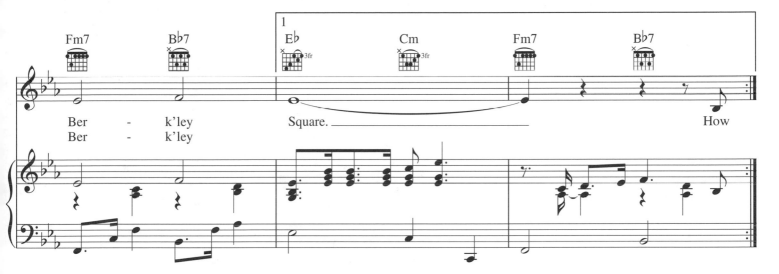

Ber - k'ley Square. _____ How
Ber - k'ley

Square. I know 'cause I was there

that night in Ber - k'ley Square. _____

# NORWEGIAN WOOD
## (This Bird Has Flown)

Words and Music by JOHN LENNON
and PAUL McCARTNEY

# ON A SLOW BOAT TO CHINA

By FRANK LOESSER

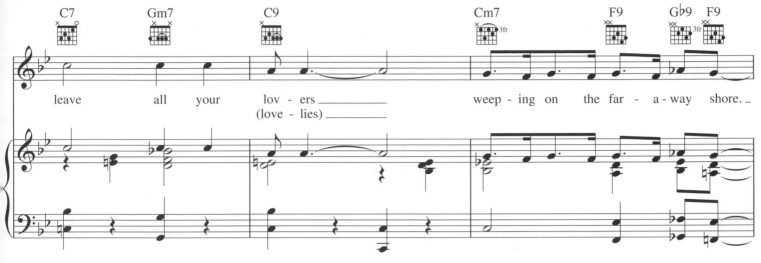

leave all your lov - ers _____ weep - ing on the far - a - way shore. _
(love - lies) _____

_____ Out on the brin - y _____ with a moon big and

shin - y, _____ melt - ing your heart _____ of stone, _____

_____ I'd love to get you _____ on a slow boat to

# ONE FOR MY BABY
## (And One More for the Road)
### from the Motion Picture THE SKY'S THE LIMIT

Lyric by JOHNNY MERCER
Music by HAROLD ARLEN

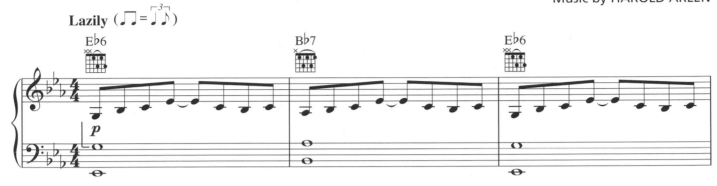

It's quar-ter to three. There's no one in the place ex-

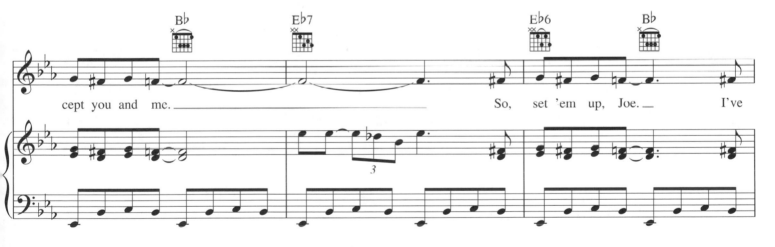

cept you and me. So, set 'em up, Joe. I've

got a lit-tle sto-ry you ought-a know. We're

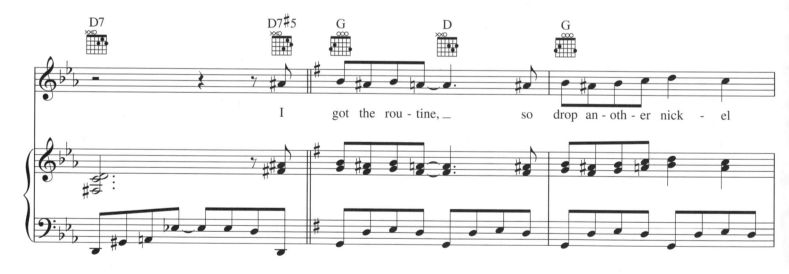

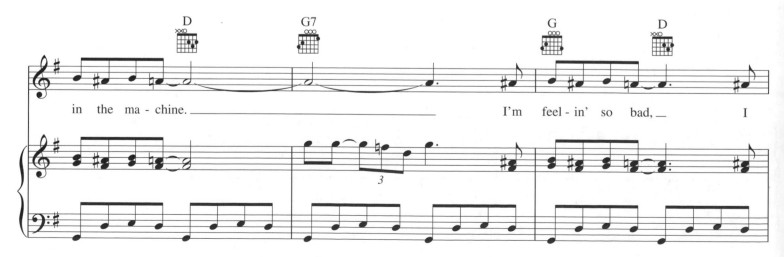

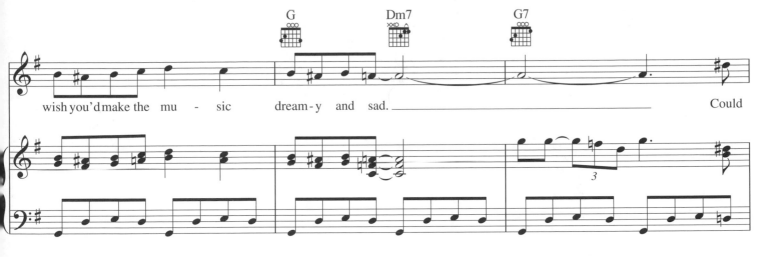

wish you'd make the mu - sic dream-y and sad. _____ Could

tell you a lot, ___ but you've got ___ to be true to your code. ___

Make it one for my ba - by and one more for the road.

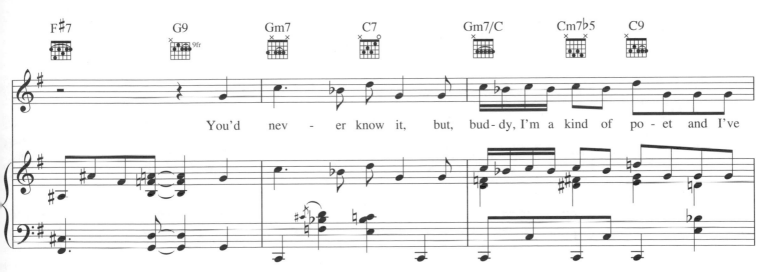

You'd nev - er know it, but, bud-dy, I'm a kind of po-et and I've

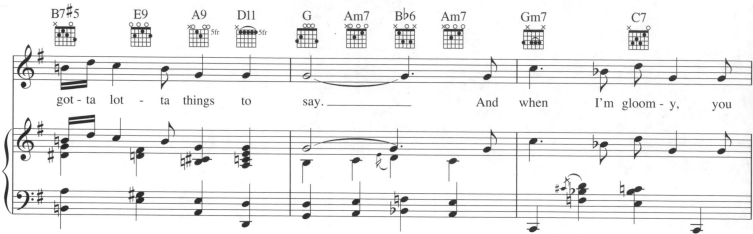

got-ta lot-ta things to say._____ And when I'm gloom-y, you

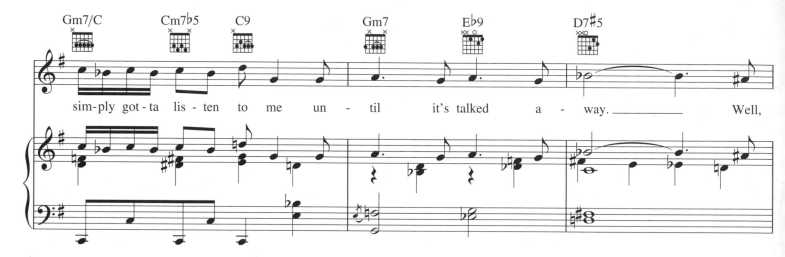

sim-ply got-ta lis-ten to me un-til it's talked a-way._____ Well,

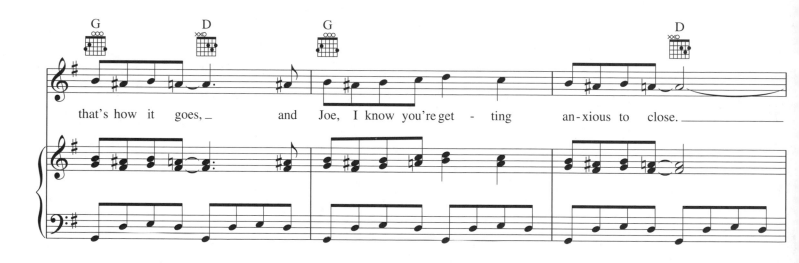

that's how it goes,_ and Joe, I know you're get-ting an-xious to close._____

_____ So, thanks for the cheer._ I hope you did-n't mind my

# OUT OF NOWHERE

## from the Paramount Picture DUDE RANCH

Words by EDWARD HEYMAN
Music by JOHNNY GREEN

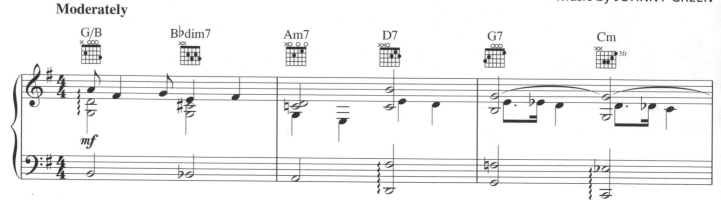

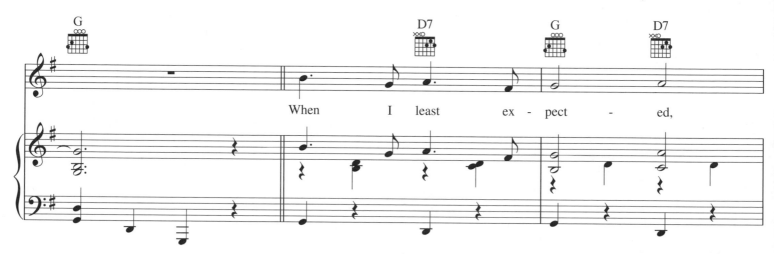

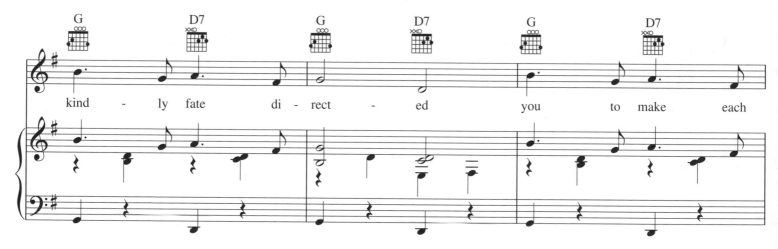

When I least ex-pect-ed, kind-ly fate di-rect-ed you to make each

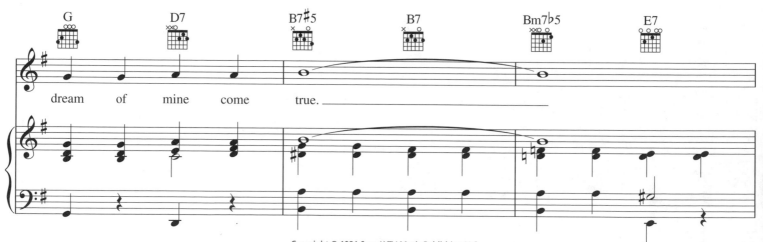

dream of mine come true. ___

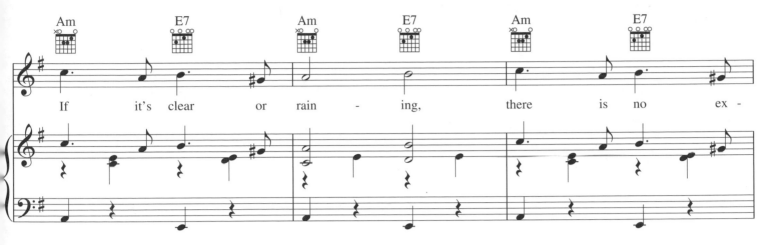

If it's clear or rain - ing, there is no ex -

plain - ing, things just hap - pen and so did

you. _____ You came to me _____

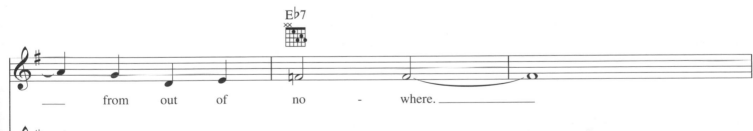

_____ from out of no - where. _____

You took my heart _____ and found it free. _____

__ Won - der - ful dreams, __ won - der - ful schemes __ from

no - where, made ev -'ry hour sweet as a flow - er for

me. _____ If you should go _____ back to your

no - where, _____ leav-ing me with _____ a mem - o -

ry, _____ I'll al - ways wait \_\_\_ for your re - turn out of

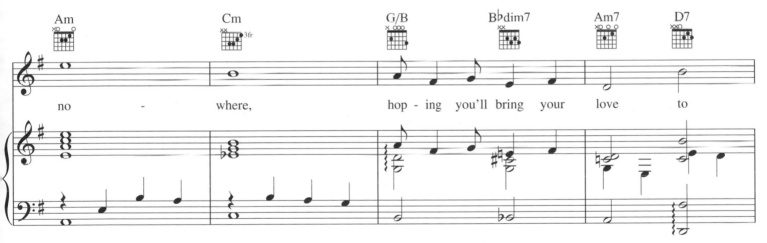

no - where, hop - ing you'll bring your love to

me. me. \_\_\_\_\_

# PERDIDO

Words by HARRY LENK and ERVIN DRAKE
Music by JUAN TIZOL

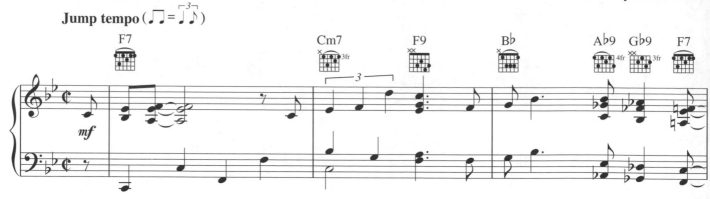

le - ro, _____ she glanced as she danced a Bo - le - ro. _____ I

said, tak - ing off my som - bre - ro, _____ "Let's meet for a sweet si -

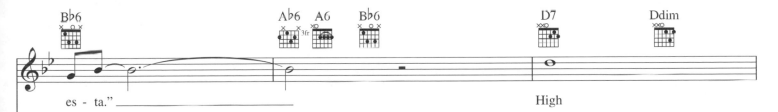

es - ta." _____ High

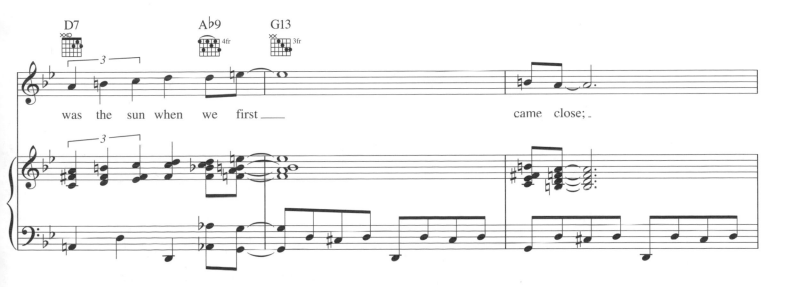

was the sun when we first ___ came close; _

low was the moon when we said, ___

"A - dios!" ___ Per - di - do ___ since then has my heart been per -

di - do ___ I know I must go to Tor - ri - do ___ that

yearn - ing to lose per - di - do. ___

# POLKA DOTS AND MOONBEAMS

Words by JOHNNY BURKE
Music by JIMMY VAN HEUSEN

# PRELUDE TO A KISS

Words by IRVING GORDON and IRVING MILLS
Music by DUKE ELLINGTON

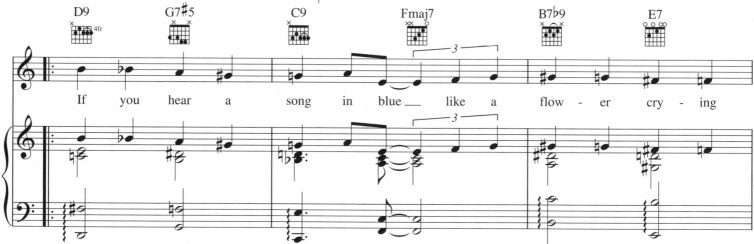

If you hear a song in blue ___ like a flow-er cry-ing

for the dew, ___ that was my heart ser-e-nad-ing you, ___

# THE RAINBOW CONNECTION
## from THE MUPPET MOVIE

Words and Music by PAUL WILLIAMS
and KENNETH L. ASCHER

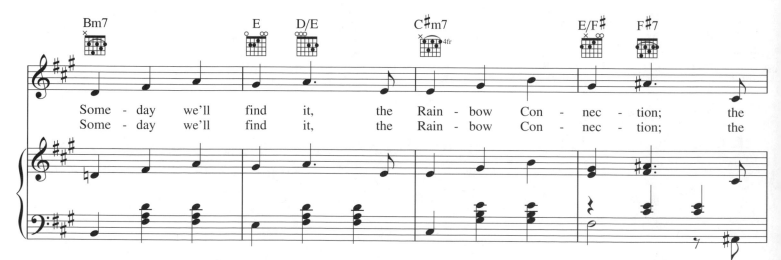

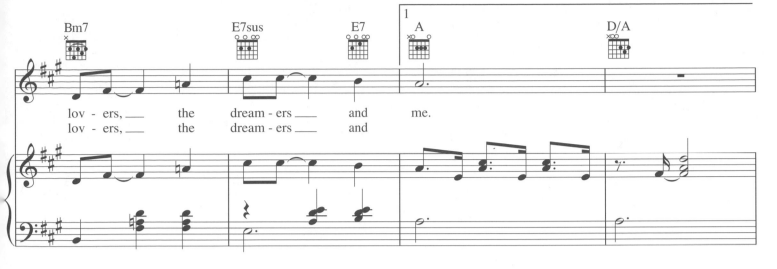

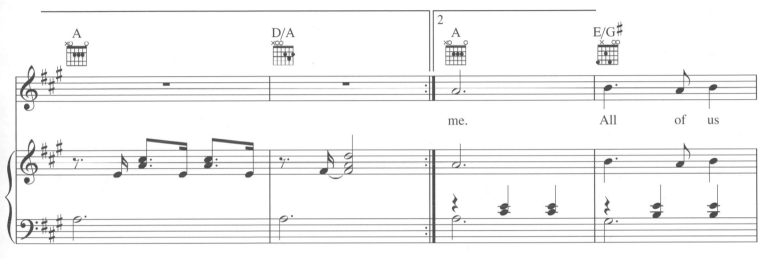

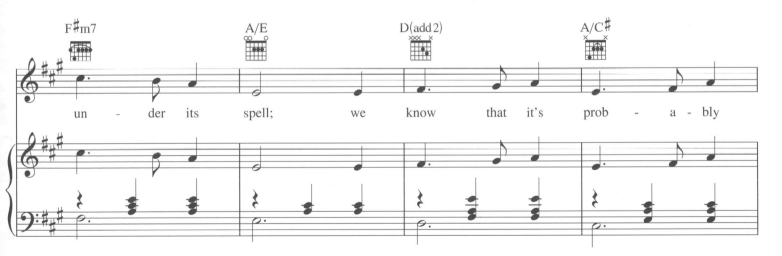

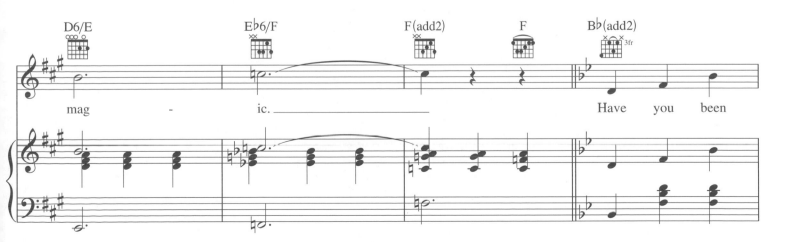

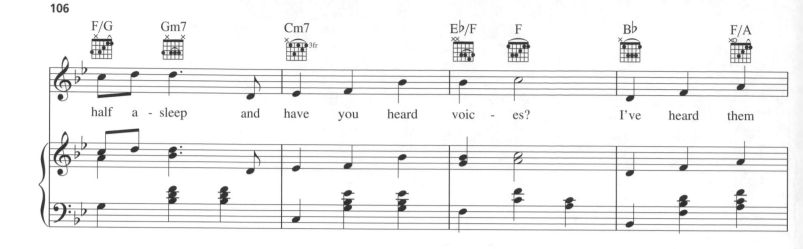

half a-sleep and have you heard voic-es? I've heard them

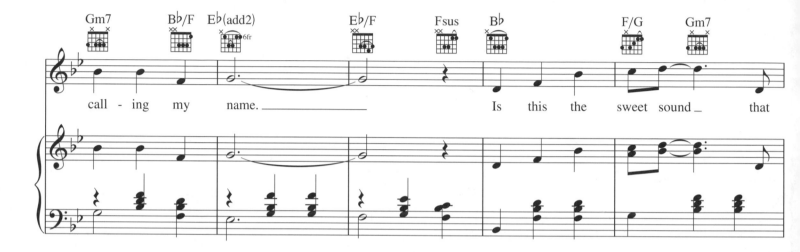

call-ing my name._____ Is this the sweet sound __ that

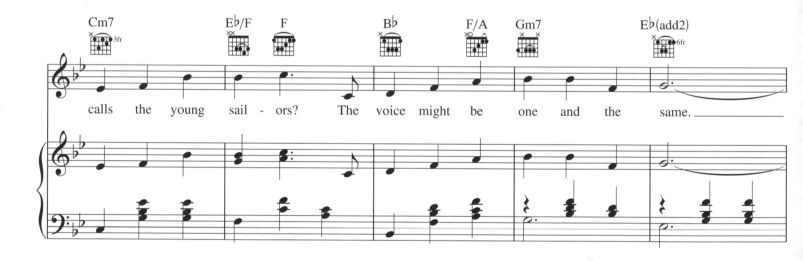

calls the young sail-ors? The voice might be one and the same._____

__ I've heard it too man-y times to ig-

nore it. It's some-thing that I'm s'posed to be. ___

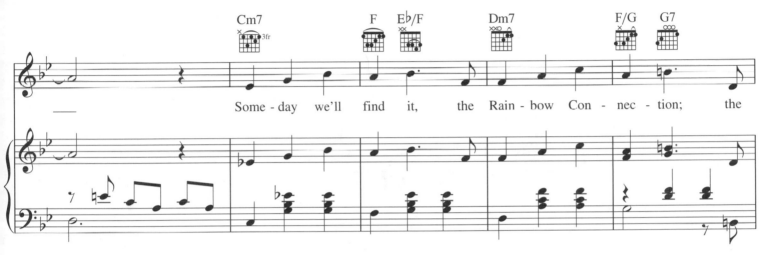

Some-day we'll find it, the Rain-bow Con-nec-tion; the

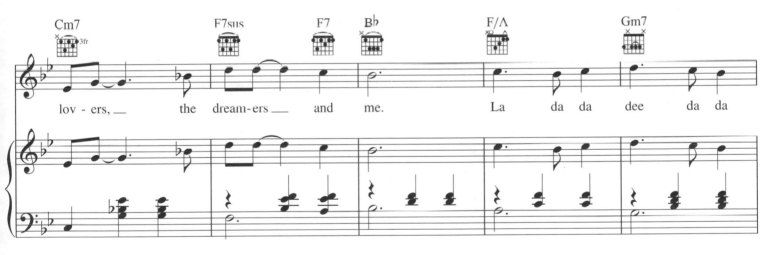

lov-ers, ___ the dream-ers ___ and me. La da da dee da da

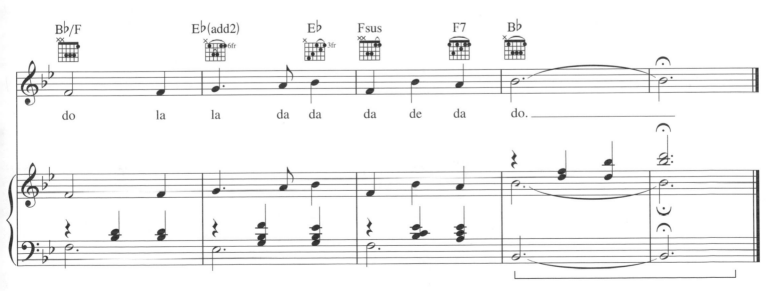

do la la da da da de da do. ___

# PUTTIN' ON THE RITZ

## from the Motion Picture PUTTIN' ON THE RITZ

Words and Music by
IRVING BERLIN

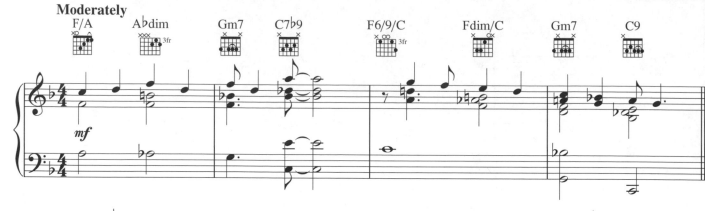

Have you seen the well-to-do up and down Park

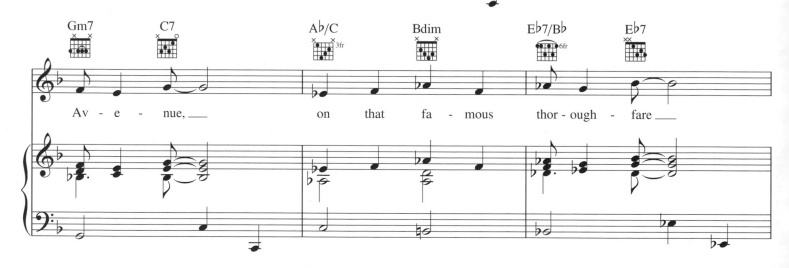

Av-e-nue, on that fa-mous thor-ough-fare

with their nos-es in the air. High hats and

# ROCKIN' CHAIR

Words and Music by
HOAGY CARMICHAEL

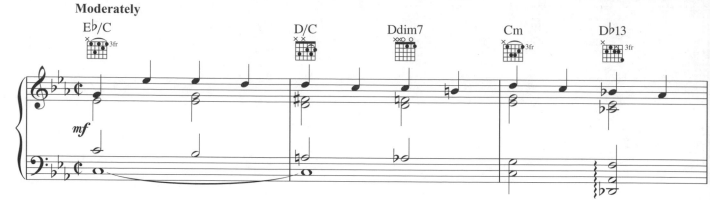

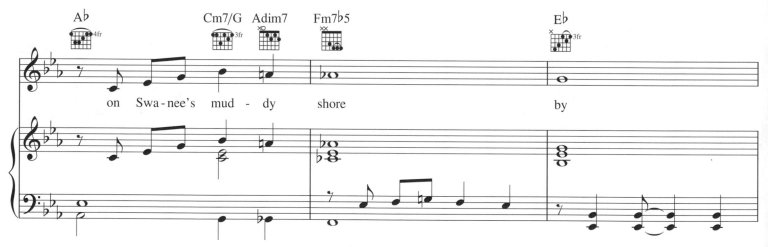

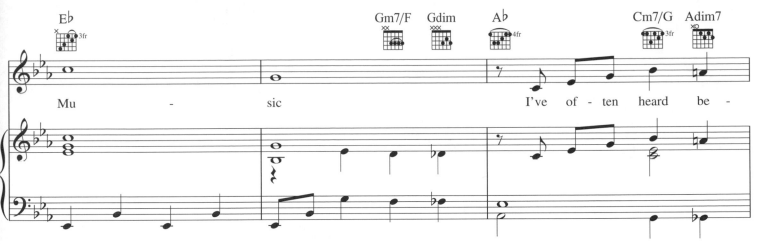

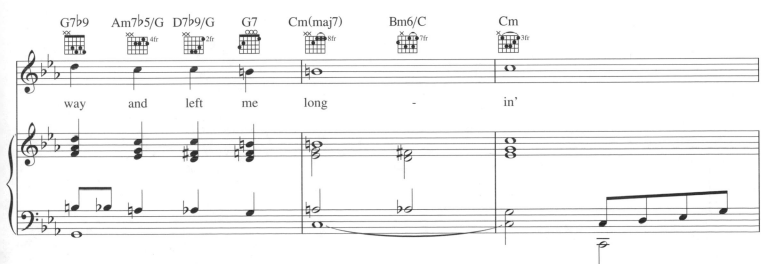

Can't get from this cab- in, _____ goin' no -

where; just sit me here grab - bin' at the

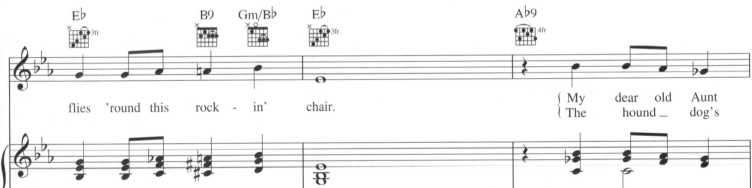

flies 'round this rock - in' chair.

My dear old Aunt
The hound _ dog's

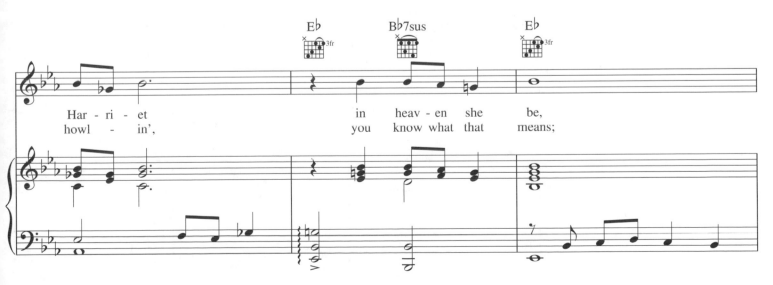

Har - ri - et
howl - in',

in heav - en she be,
you know what that means;

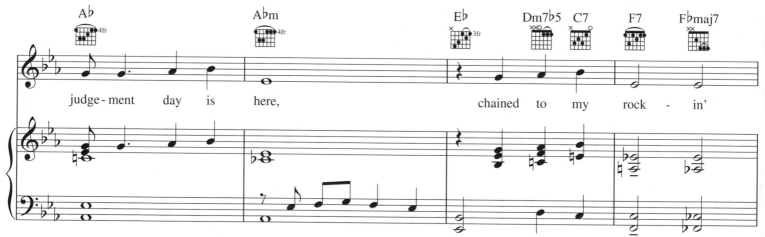

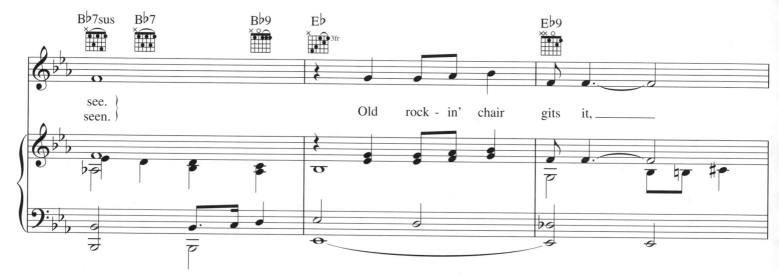

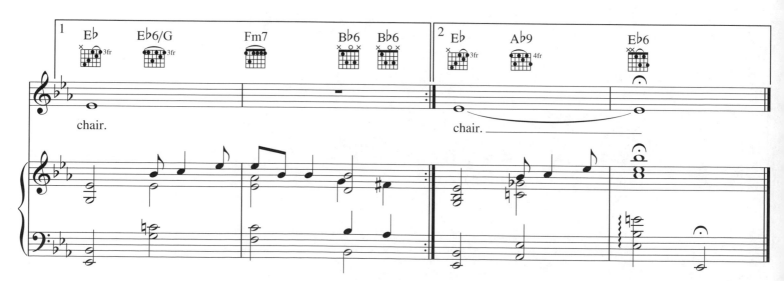

# SENTIMENTAL JOURNEY

Words and Music by BUD GREEN,
LES BROWN and BEN HOMER

Ev - 'ry roll-ing stone gets to feel a - lone when home, sweet home is far a - way. ___

I'm a roll-ing stone who's been so a - lone un - til to - day.

Gon - na take a sen - ti - men - tal jour-ney, gon - na set my

heart at ease. \_ Gon - na make a sen - ti - men - tal jour-ney to re-new old

mem - o - ries. \_ Got my bag, I got my res - er - va-tion, spent each dime I

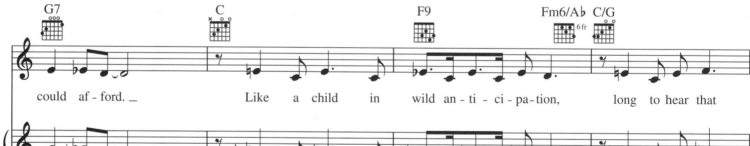

could af - ford. \_ Like a child in wild an - ti - ci - pa-tion, long to hear that

"All \_\_ a - board." \_ Sev - en, \_\_ that's the time we leave, at

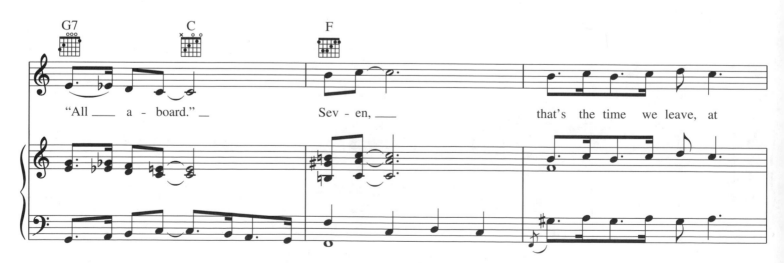

# ROUTE 66

By BOBBY TROUP

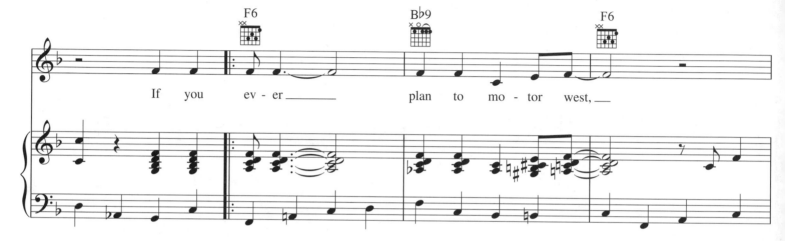

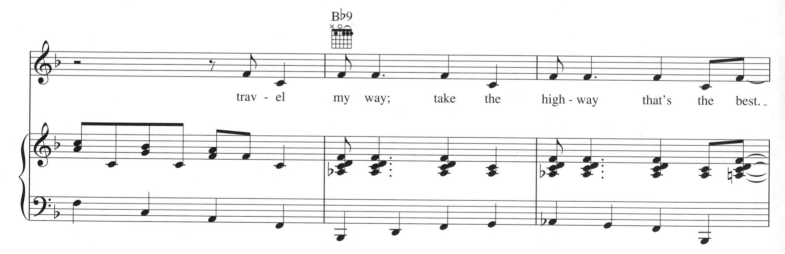

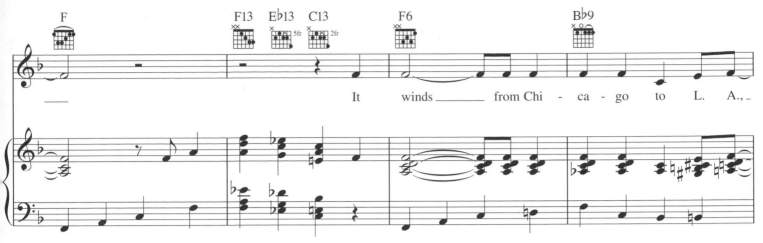

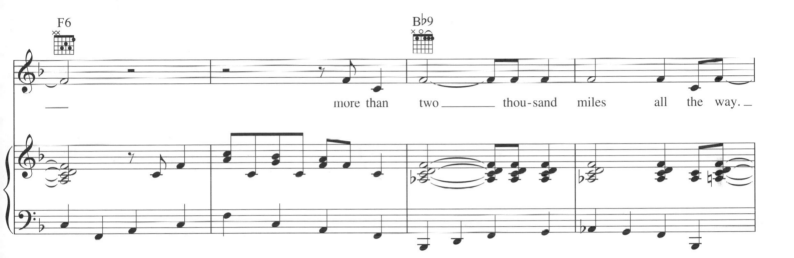

O-kla-ho-ma Cit-y is might - y pret - ty. You'll see ___ Am - a -

ril - lo, ___ Gal - lup, New Mex - i - co, ___ Flag-staff, Ar - i - zo - na;

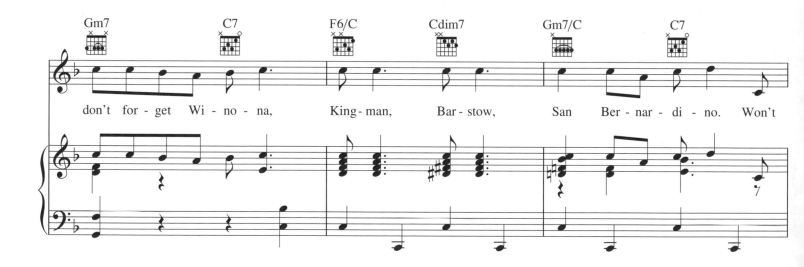

don't for-get Wi - no - na, King - man, Bar - stow, San Ber - nar - di - no. Won't

you ___ get hip to this time - ly tip: ___

When you _____ make that Cal - i - for - nia trip, _____

_____ get your kicks on Route Six - ty Six! _____

_____ If you _____ Get your

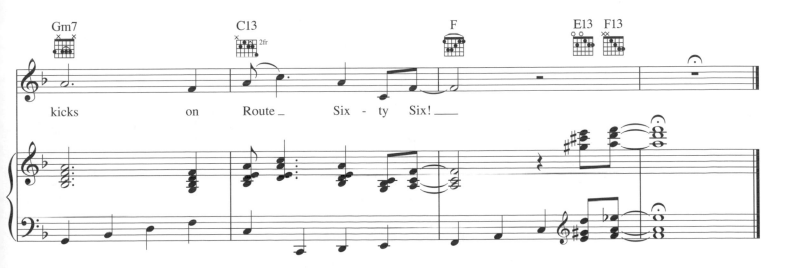

kicks on Route _____ Six - ty Six! _____

# SENTIMENTAL ME

## from the Broadway Musical THE GARRICK GAIETIES

Words by LORENZ HART
Music by RICHARD RODGERS

Look at me a-gain, dear; Let's hold hands and then, dear, sigh in
Dar - ling you're to hand - some, strong and clev - er and some - times you

cho - rus; It won't bore us, to be sure; _____
seem, dear, like a dream, dear, that came true. _____

There's no mean - ing to it, yet we o - ver - do it, with a
That's why I picked you out; Bet - ter men I threw out of my

rel - ish that is hell - ish to en - dure.
liv - ing room while giv - ing room to you.

I am not the kind that mere - ly flirts;
I would rath - er read of love in books;

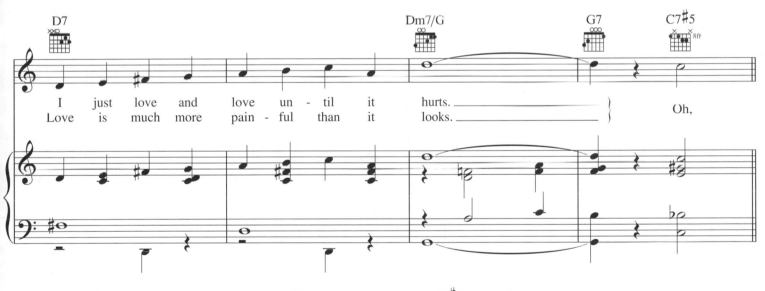

I just love and love un - til it hurts.
Love is much more pain - ful than it looks. Oh,

sen - ti - men - tal me and poor ro - man - tic you;

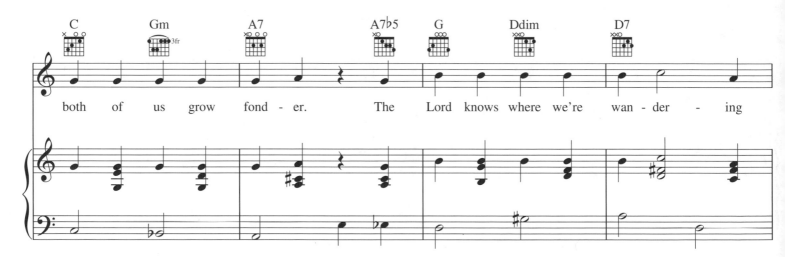

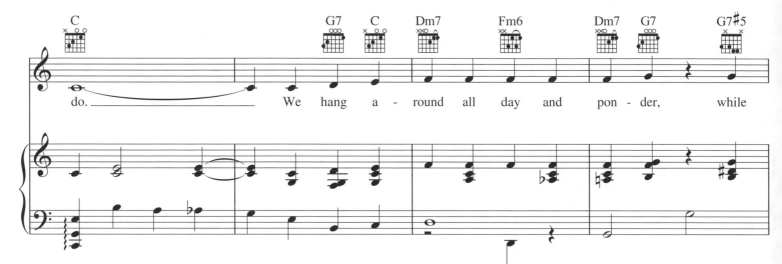

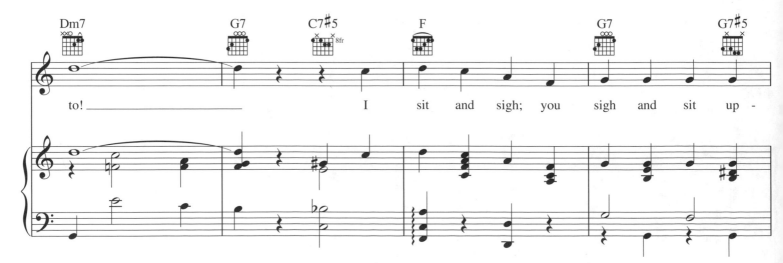

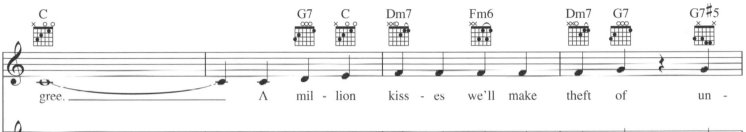

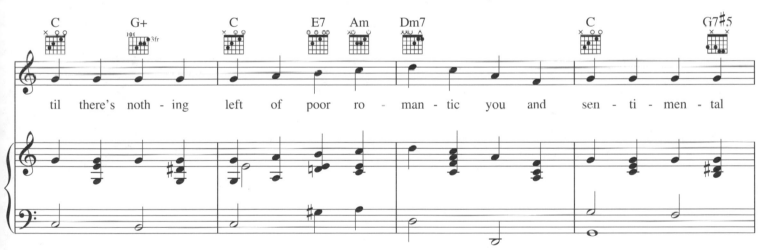

# SKYLARK

Words by JOHNNY MERCER
Music by HOAGY CARMICHAEL

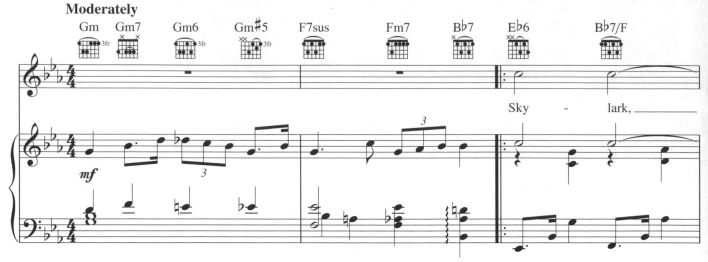

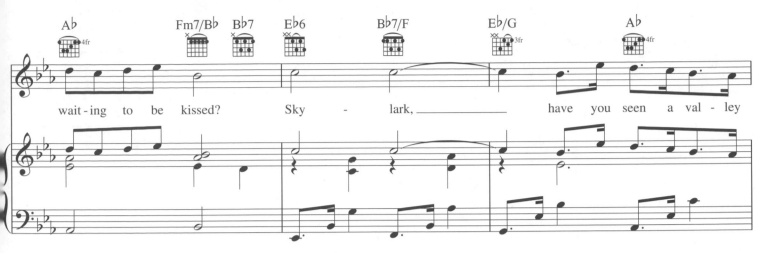

wait-ing to be kissed? Sky - lark, _____ have you seen a val - ley

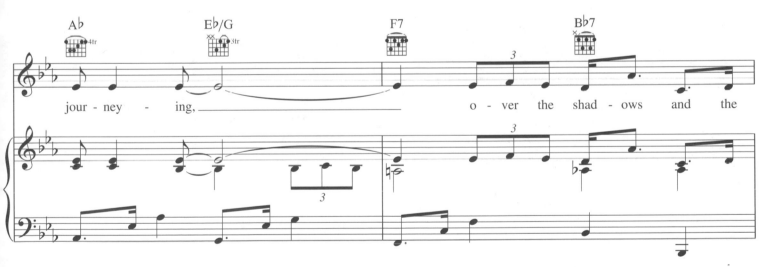

green with spring, _____ where my heart can go a -

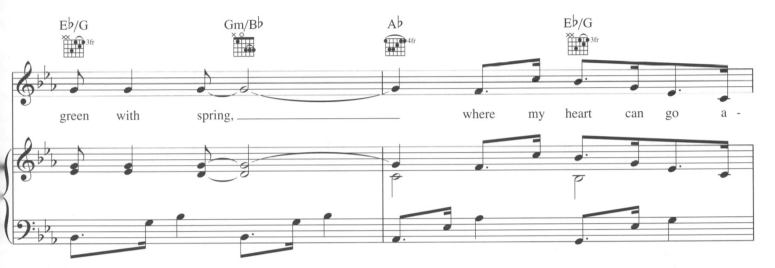

jour - ney - ing, _____ o - ver the shad - ows and the

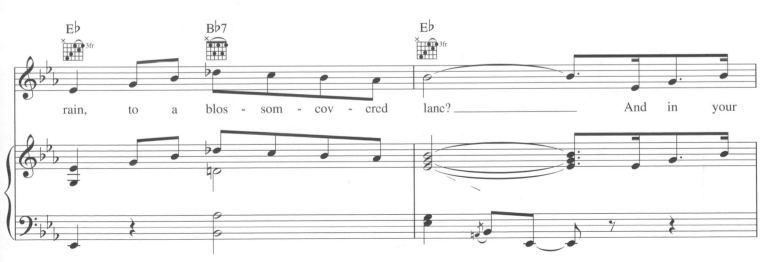

rain, to a blos - som - cov - ered lane? _____ And in your

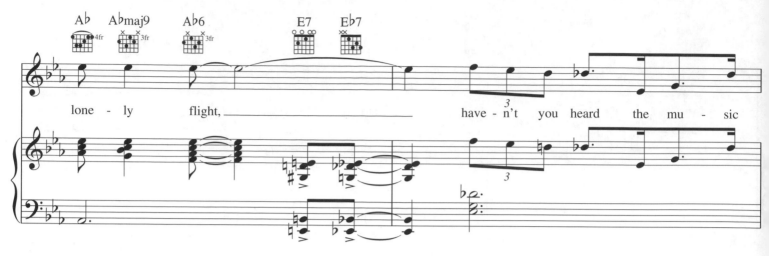

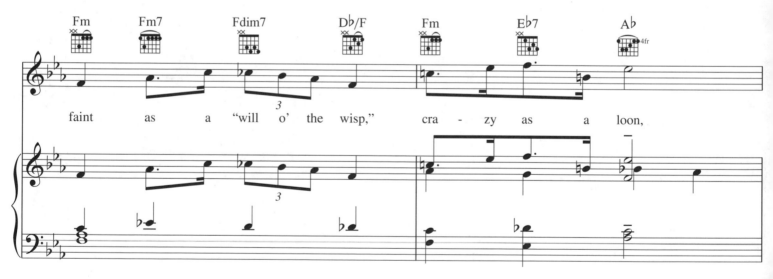

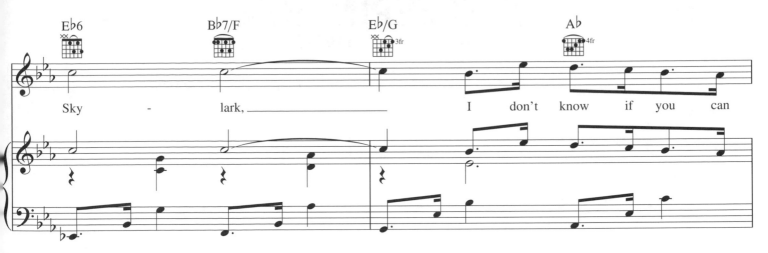

Sky - lark, _____ I don't know if you can

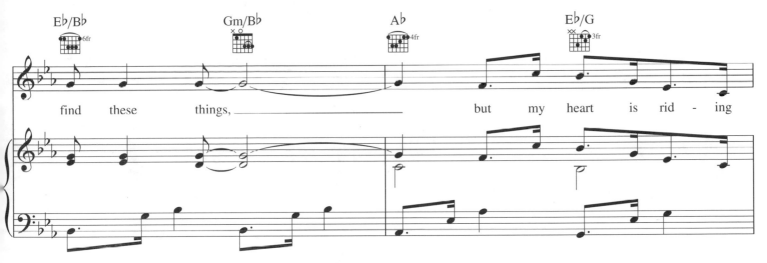

find these things, _____ but my heart is rid - ing

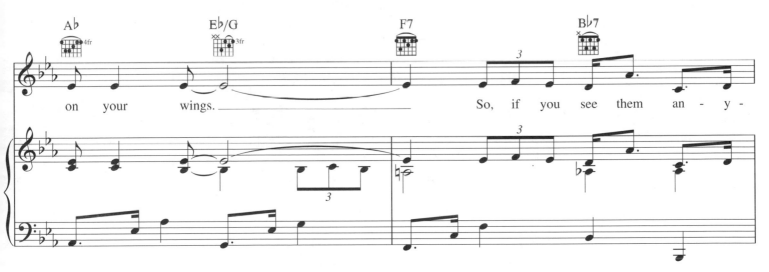

on your wings. _____ So, if you see them an - y -

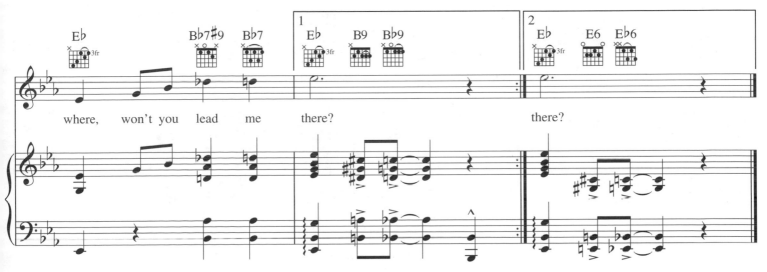

where, won't you lead me there? there?

# A SLEEPIN' BEE

## from HOUSE OF FLOWERS

Lyric by TRUMAN CAPOTE and HAROLD ARLEN
Music by HAROLD ARLEN

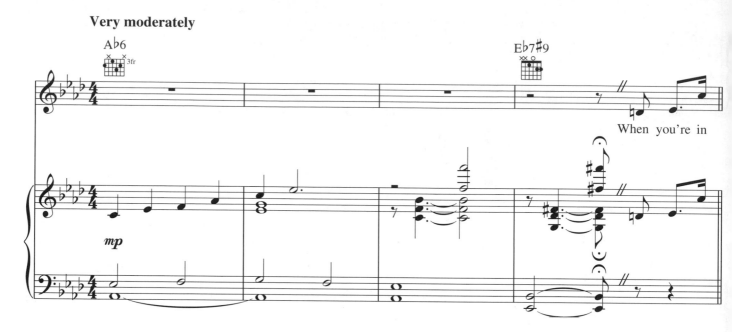

**Very moderately**

When you're in

love and you are won-d'rin' if he real-ly is the one, there's an

an-cient sign sure to tell___ you if your search is o-ver and done. Catch a

bee and if he don't sting you, you're in a spell that's just be - gun. It's a

guar - an - tee 'til the end of time your true love you have won, have

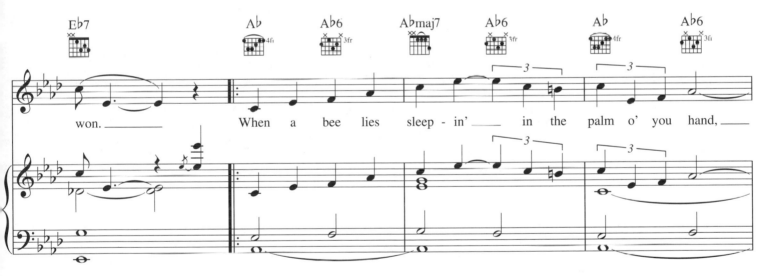

won. _____ When a bee lies sleep - in' _____ in the palm o' you hand, _____

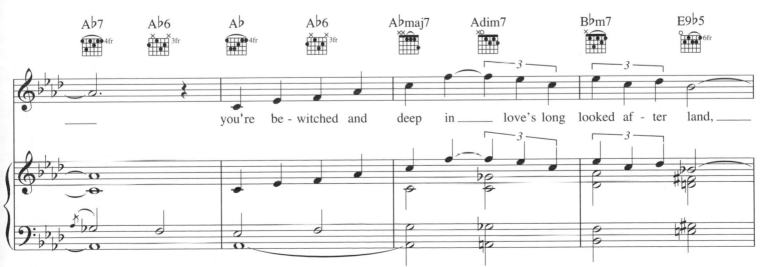

_____ you're be - witched and deep in _____ love's long looked af - ter land, _____

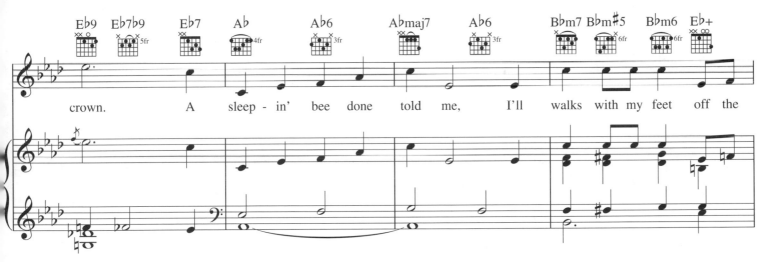

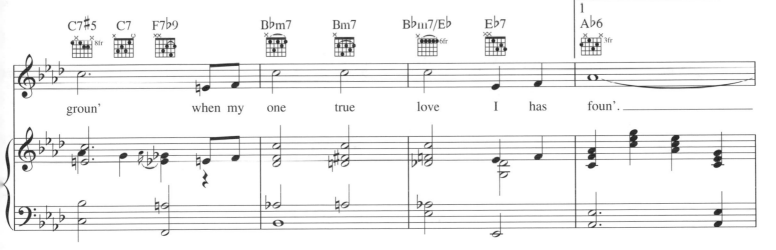

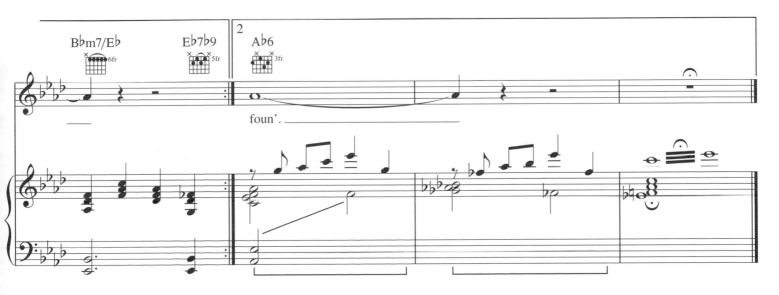

# SMALL FRY

### from the Paramount Picture SING, YOU SINNERS

Words by FRANK LOESSER
Music by HOAGY CARMICHAEL

**Slowly and lazily**

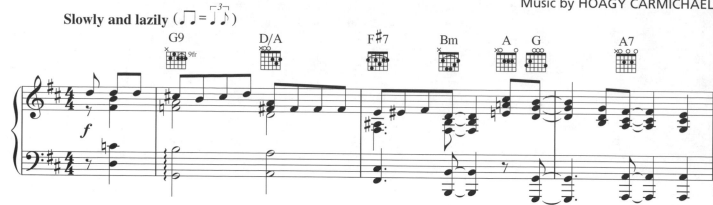

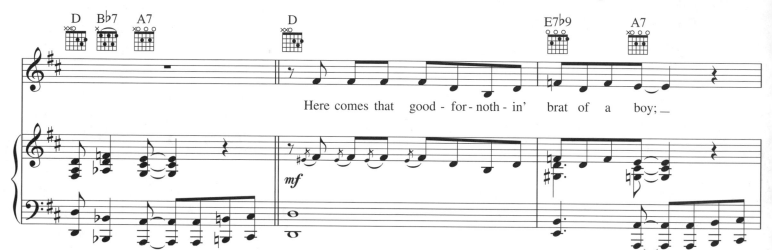

Here comes that good-for-noth-in' brat of a boy; —

he's such a dev-il I could whip him with joy. —

He's been ca-rous-in' at the bur-ley-cue. —

peck - in' all day long to some old ra - di - o song. ___ Oh! yes,
feet all soak - in' wet, you'll be the death of me yet. ___ Oh! me,

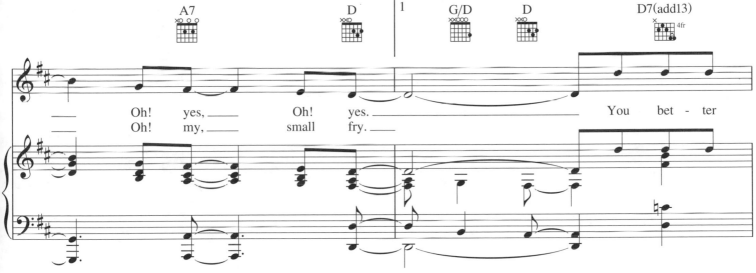

___ Oh! yes, ___ Oh! yes. _____ You bet - ter
Oh! my, ___ small fry. ___

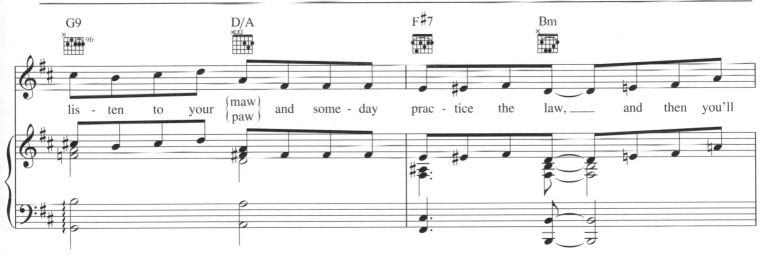

lis - ten to your {maw/paw} and some - day prac - tice the law, ___ and then you'll

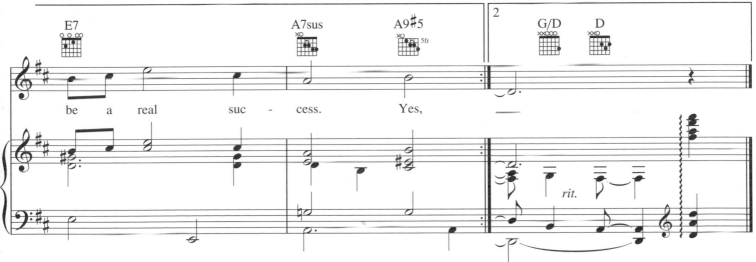

be a real suc - cess. Yes,

# SOFTLY AS IN A MORNING SUNRISE

## from THE NEW MOON

Lyrics by OSCAR HAMMERSTEIN II
Music by SIGMUND ROMBERG

**Moderate Tango**

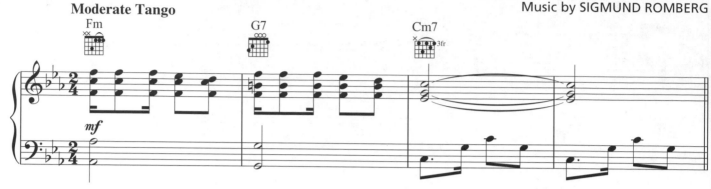

Love came to me, gay and ten - der. Love came to me, sweet sur - ren - der.

Love came to me _____ in bright ro - man - tic splen - dor.

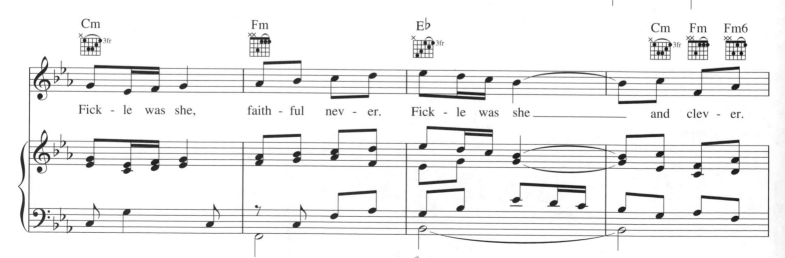

Fick - le was she, faith - ful nev - er. Fick - le was she _____ and clev - er.

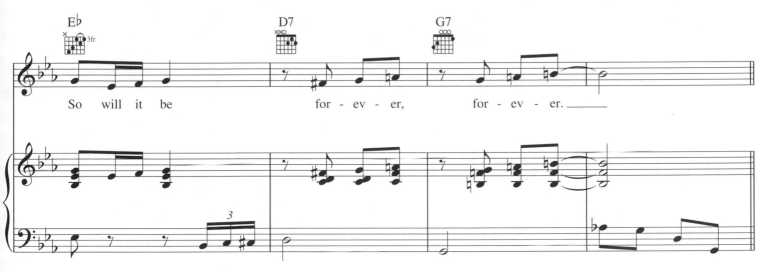

So will it be for - ev - er, for - ev - er.____

Soft - ly, as in a morn - ing sun - rise, the light of love comes

steal - ing in - to a new-born day, oh!

Flam - ing with all the glow of sun - rise,

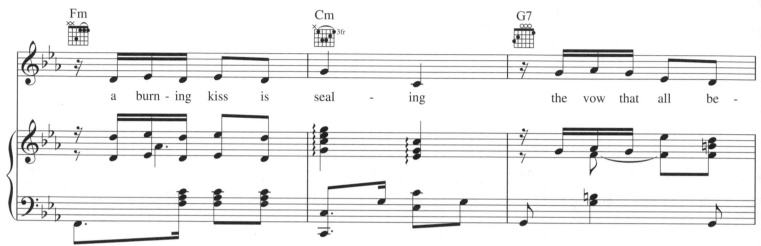

a burn - ing kiss is seal - ing the vow that all be -

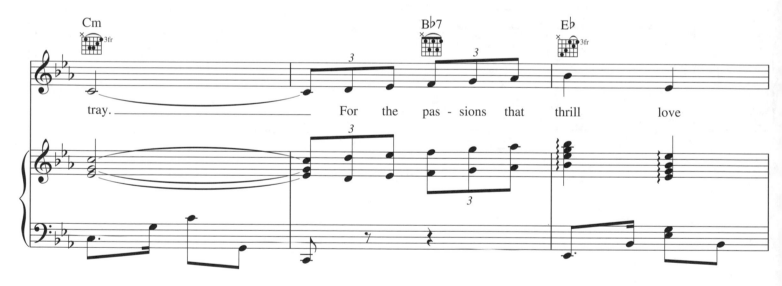

tray. _____ For the pas - sions that thrill love

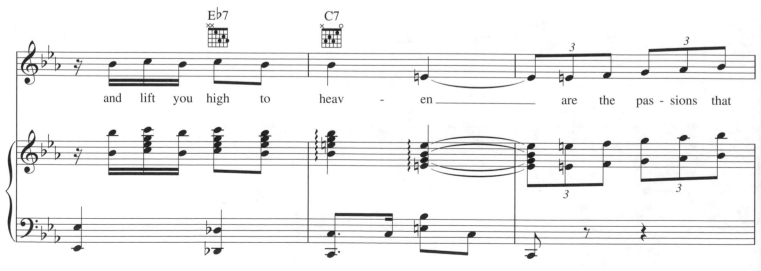

and lift you high to heav - en _____ are the pas - sions that

kill love and let you fall to hell! So

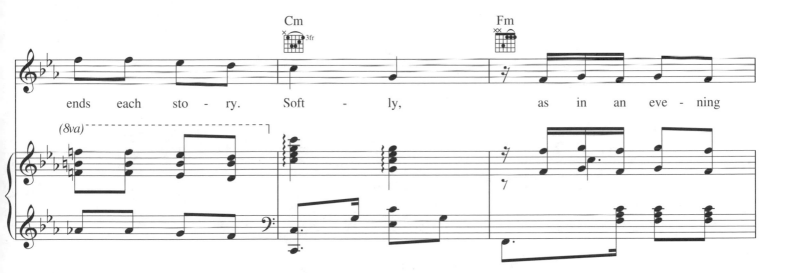

ends each sto - ry. Soft - ly, as in an eve - ning

sun - set, the light that gave you glo - ry will take it all a -

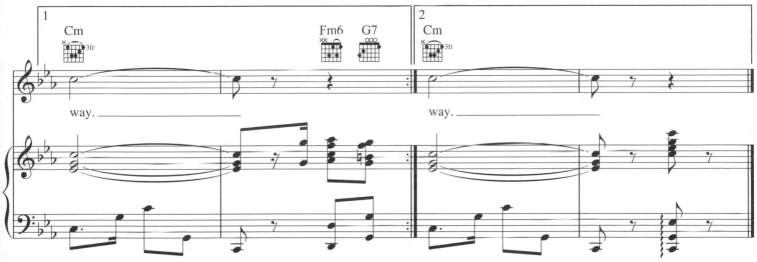

way. way.

# SOLITUDE

Words and Music by DUKE ELLINGTON,
EDDIE DE LANGE and IRVING MILLS

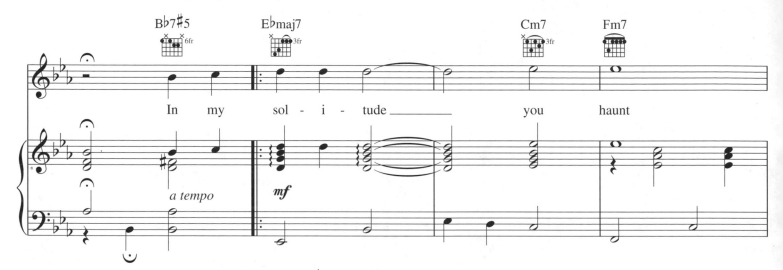

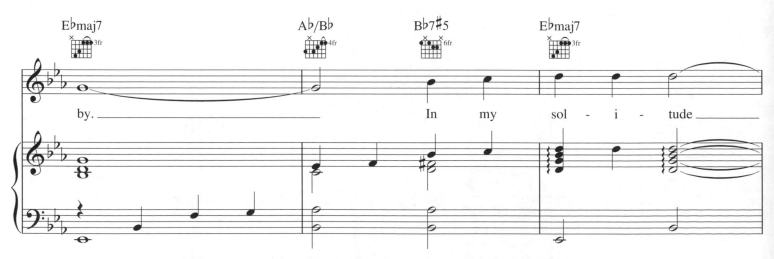

you taunt me with

mem - o - ries _____ that nev - er die. _____

_____ I sit in my chair, I'm filled with de - spair, there's

no one could be so sad. _____ With gloom ev - 'ry - where, I

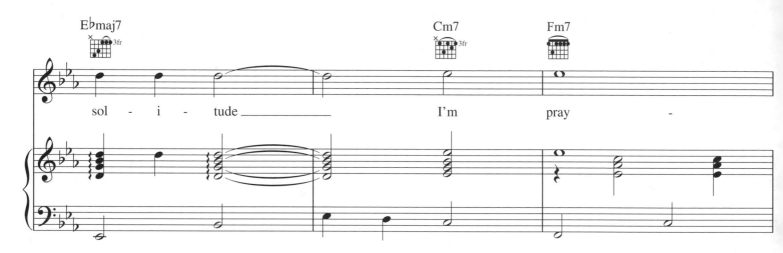

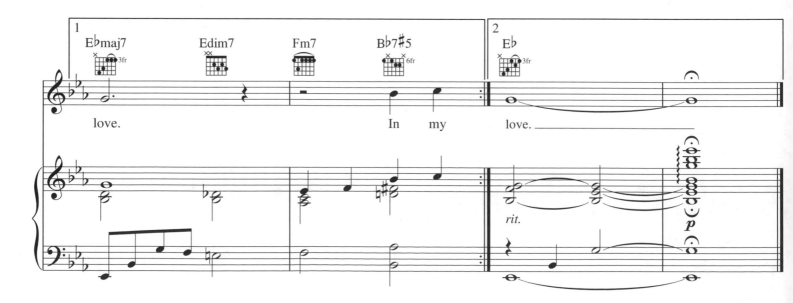

# SOPHISTICATED LADY
## from SOPHISTICATED LADIES

Words and Music by DUKE ELLINGTON,
IRVING MILLS and MITCHELL PARISH

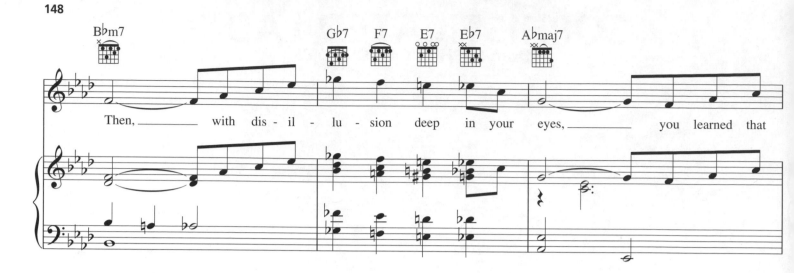

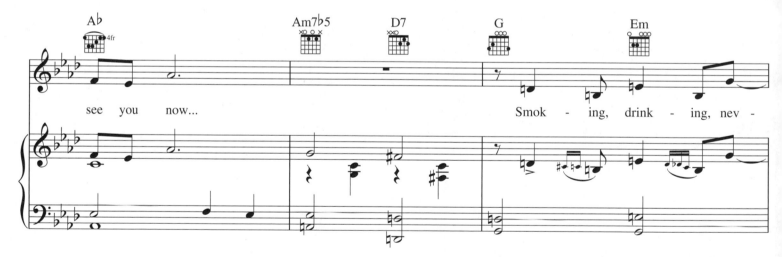

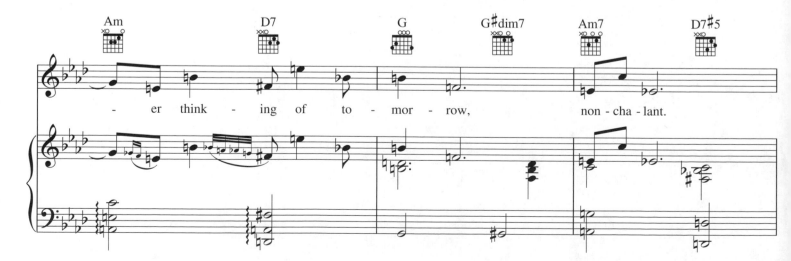

Dia - monds shin - ing, danc - - ing, din - - ing with some man in a res-tau-rant;

is that all you real - ly want? No, _____ So - phis - ti - cat - ed la - dy, I

know, _____ you miss the love you lost long a - go, _____ and when no - bod - y is nigh you

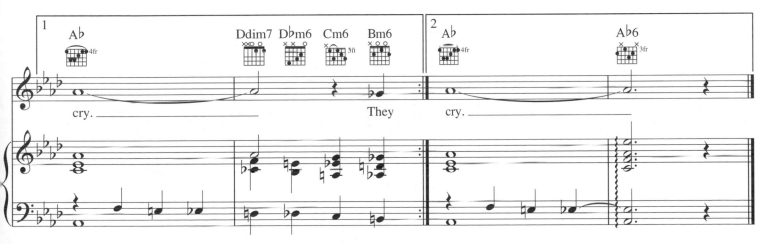

cry. _____ They cry. _____

# SOMEBODY LOVES ME
## from GEORGE WHITE'S SCANDALS OF 1924

Words by B.G. DeSYLVA and BALLARD MacDONALD
Music by GEORGE GERSHWIN
French Version by EMELIA RENAUD

may - be you were meant to be my lov - ing

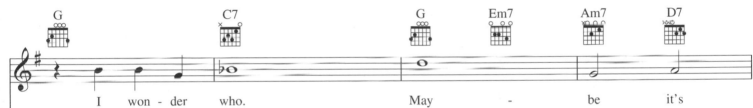

ba - by." Some - bod - y loves me,

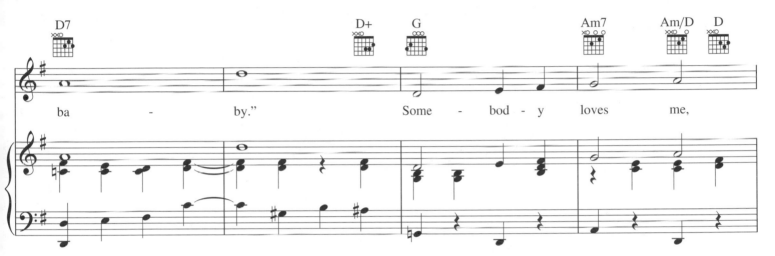

I won - der who. May - be it's

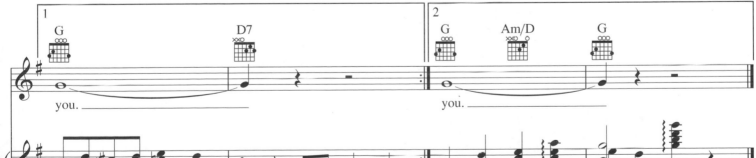

you. you.

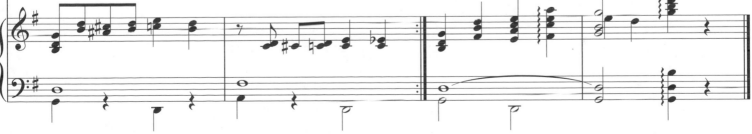

# THE SONG IS ENDED
## (But the Melody Lingers On)

Words and Music by
IRVING BERLIN

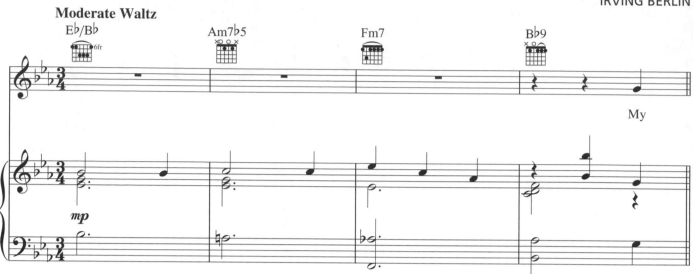

thoughts go back to a heav - en - ly dance, a

mo - ment of bliss we spent. _____ Our

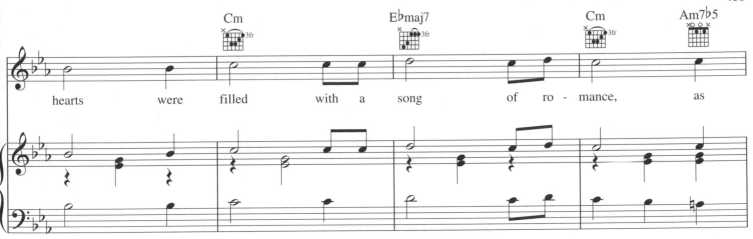

hearts were filled with a song of ro - mance, as

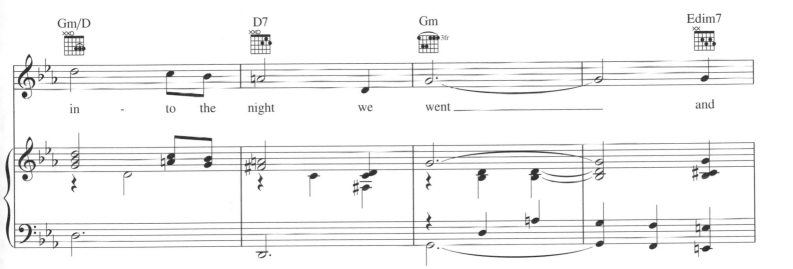

in - to the night we went _____ and

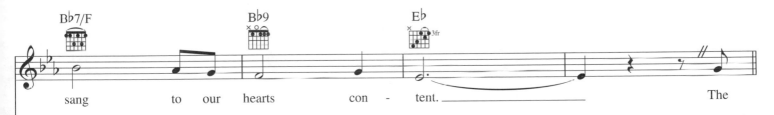

sang to our hearts con - tent. _____ The

**Moderately**

song _____ is end - ed, but the mel - o - dy lin - gers

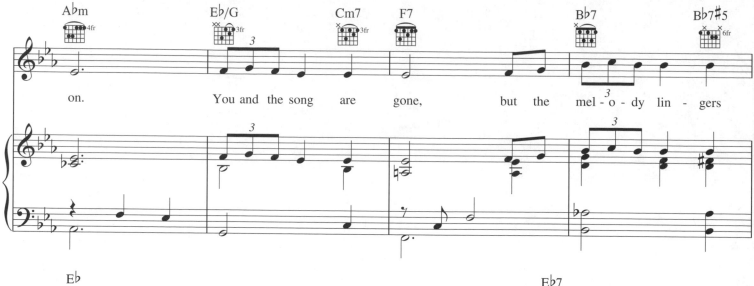

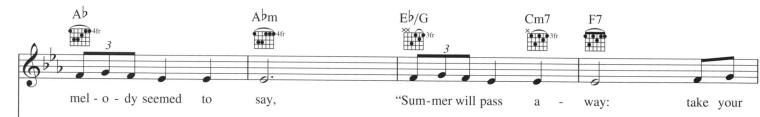

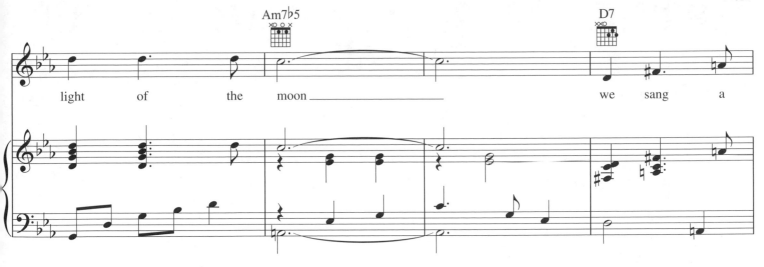

light of the moon _____ we sang a

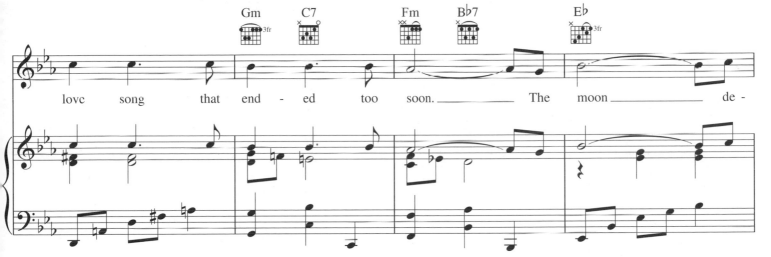

love song that end - ed too soon. _____ The moon _____ de -

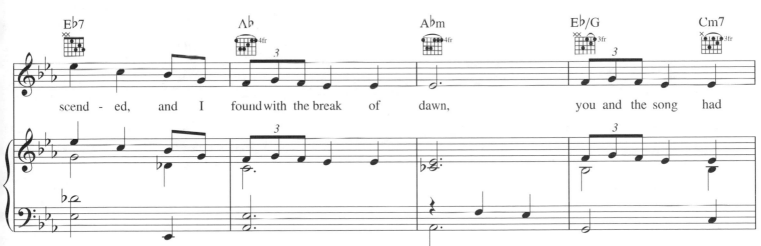

scend - ed, and I found with the break of dawn, you and the song had

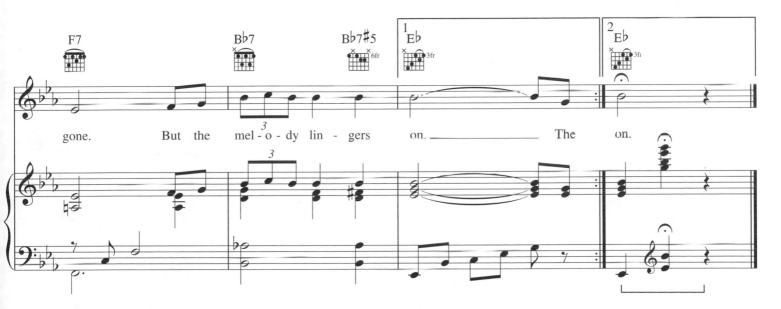

gone. But the mel - o - dy lin - gers on. _____ The on.

# SPRING CAN REALLY HANG YOU UP THE MOST

Lyric by FRAN LANDESMAN
Music by TOMMY WOLF

rived on time, on - ly what be - came of you, dear?
help a bit, my con -

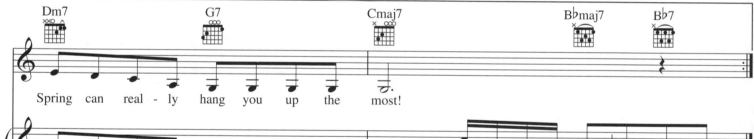

Spring can real - ly hang you up the most!

Spring can real - ly hang you up the most!

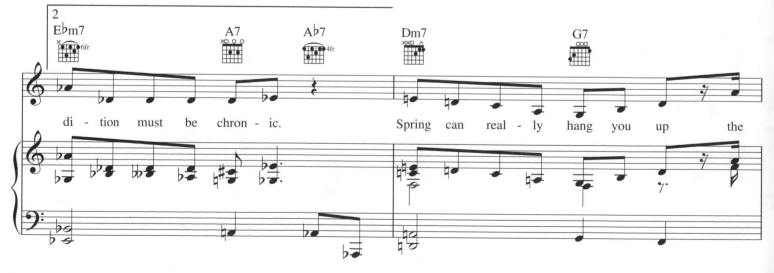

di - tion must be chron - ic. Spring can real - ly hang you up the

# SPRING WILL BE A LITTLE LATE THIS YEAR

## from the Motion Picture CHRISTMAS HOLIDAY

By FRANK LOESSER

**Moderately**

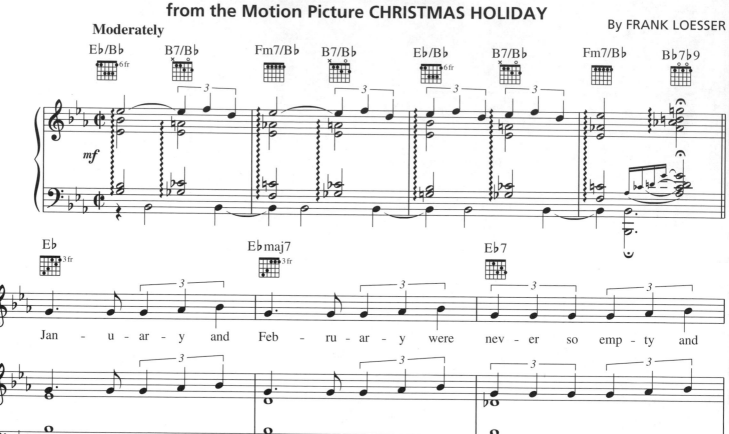

Jan - u - ar - y and Feb - ru - ar - y were nev - er so emp - ty and gray. Tra - gic - 'lly I feel like cry - ing, "With -

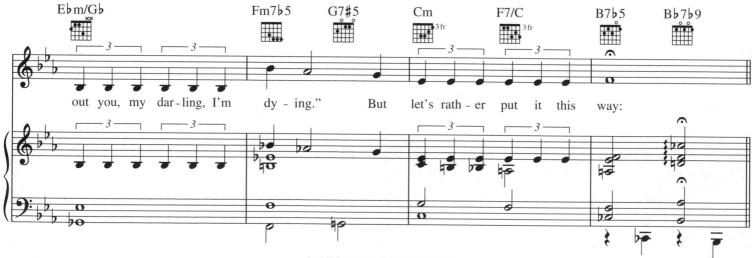

out you, my dar - ling, I'm dy - ing." But let's rath - er put it this way:

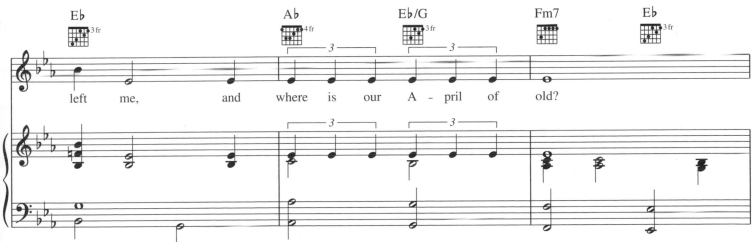

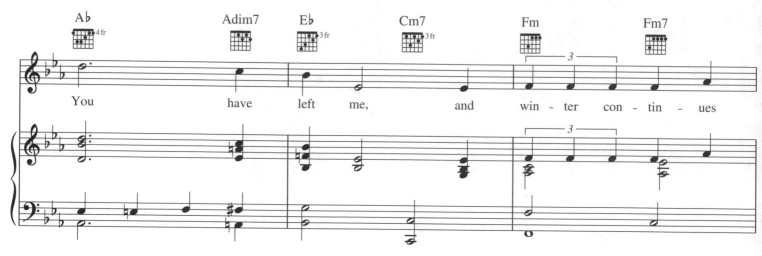

You have left me, and win - ter con - tin - ues

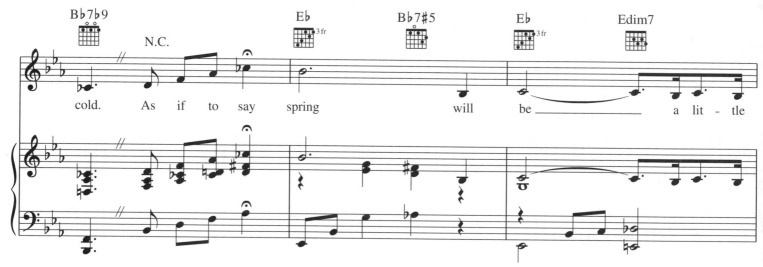

cold. As if to say spring will be _____ a lit - tle

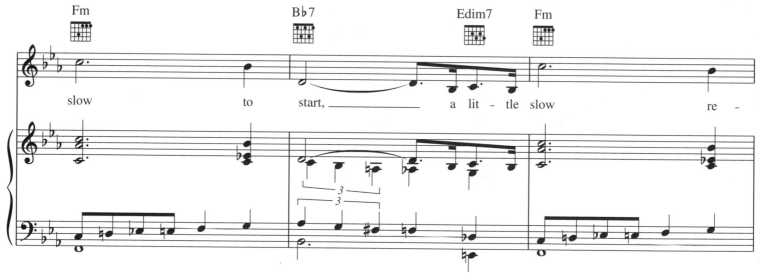

slow to start, _____ a lit - tle slow re -

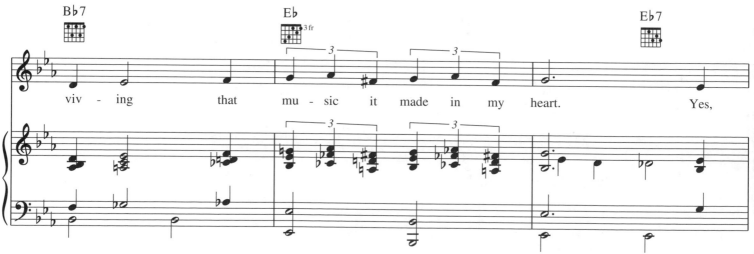

viv - ing that mu - sic it made in my heart. Yes,

time heals all things, so I need-n't cling to this

fear. It's mere-ly that spring will be _____ a lit-tle

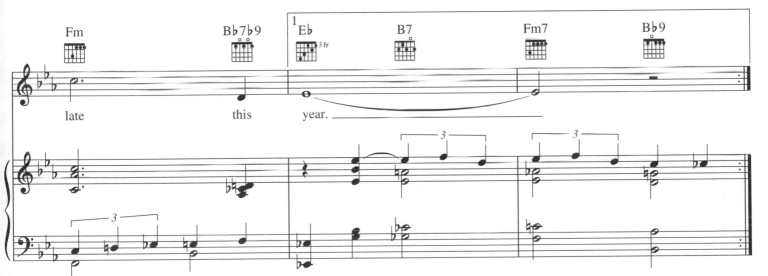

late this year. _____

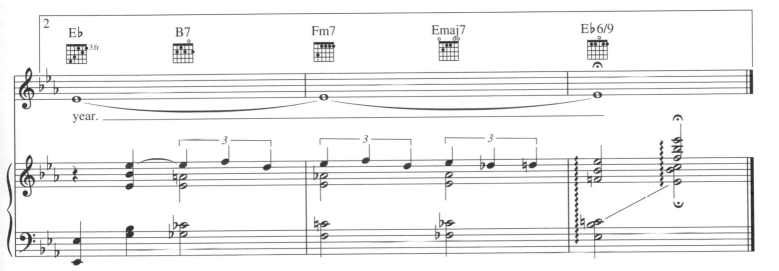

year. _____

# STARDUST

Words by MITCHELL PARISH
Music by HOAGY CARMICHAEL

won - der why I spend the lone - ly night

dream - ing of a song? The mel - o - dy haunts my rev - er - ie,

and I am once a - gain with you, _____ when our

love was new, _____ and each kiss an in - spi - ra - tion. _____

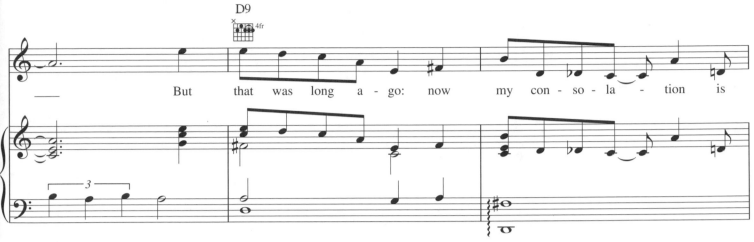

But that was long a-go: now my con-so-la-tion is

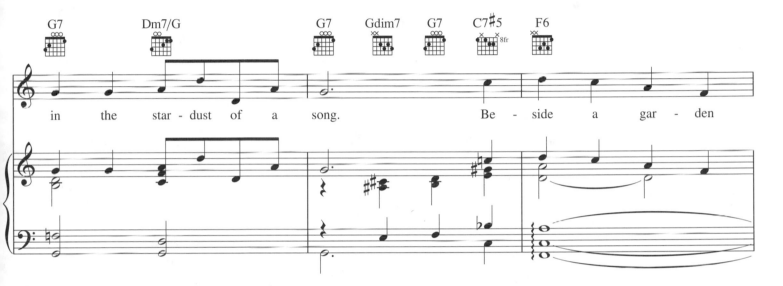

in the star-dust of a song. Be-side a gar-den

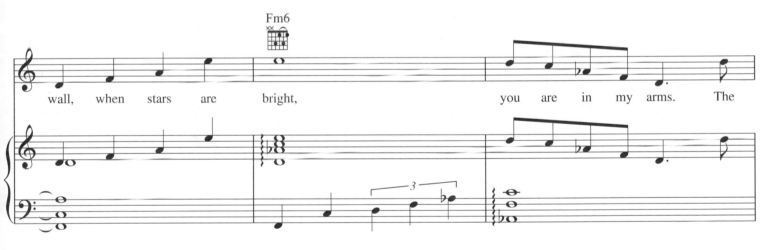

wall, when stars are bright, you are in my arms. The

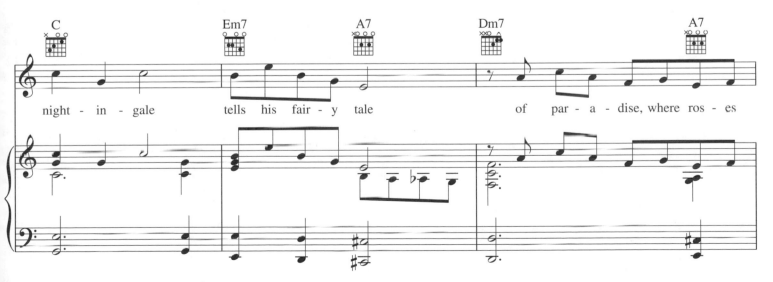

night-in-gale tells his fair-y tale of par-a-dise, where ros-es

# STELLA BY STARLIGHT

from the Paramount Picture THE UNINVITED

Words by NED WASHINGTON
Music by VICTOR YOUNG

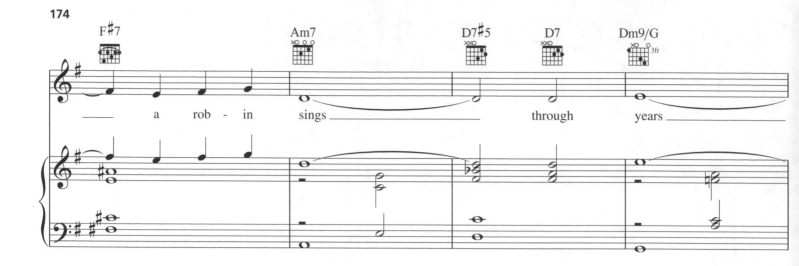

a rob - in sings _____ through years _____

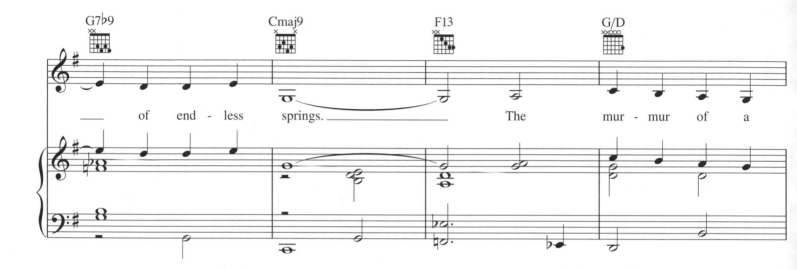

_____ of end - less springs. _____ The mur - mur of a

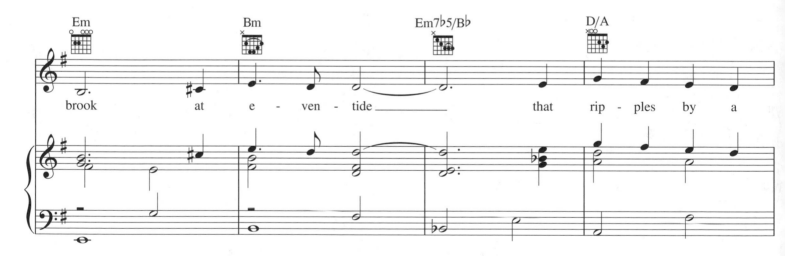

brook at e - ven - tide _____ that rip - ples by a

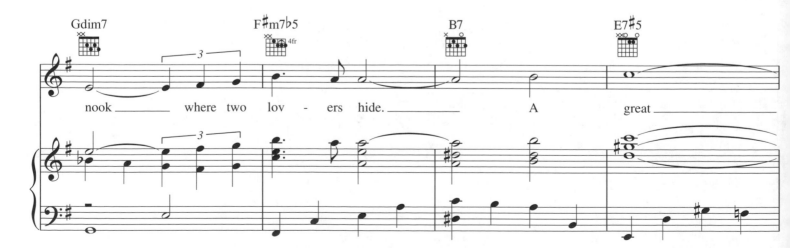

nook _____ where two lov - ers hide. _____ A great _____

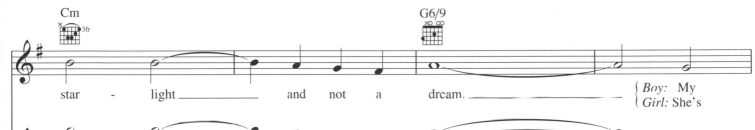

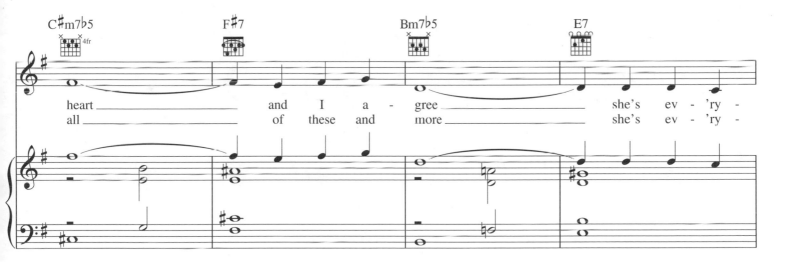

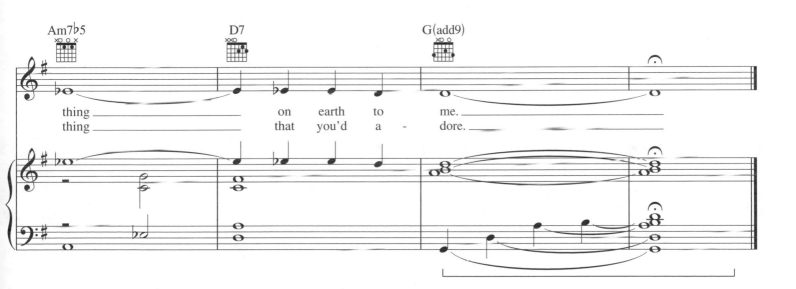

# STEPPIN' OUT WITH MY BABY

## from the Motion Picture Irving Berlin's EASTER PARADE

Words and Music by
IRVING BERLIN

Medium Jump tempo

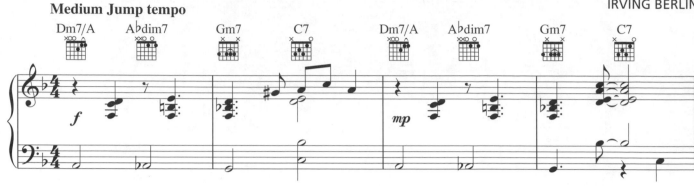

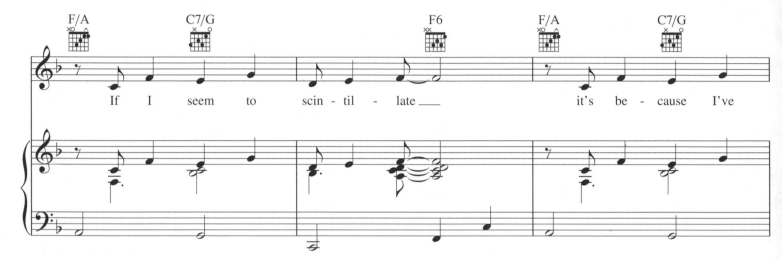

If I seem to scin - til - late ___ it's be - cause I've

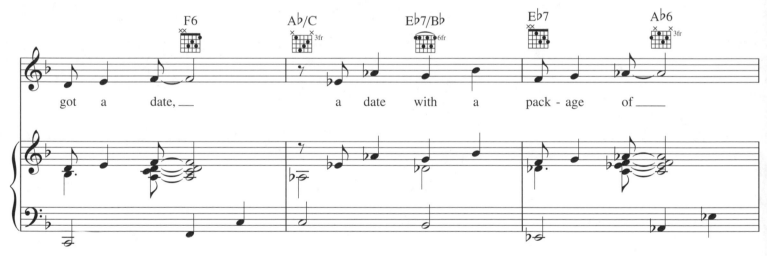

got a date, ___ a date with a pack - age of ___

the good things that come with love. ___ You don't have to

ask me, ___ I won't waste your time. But if you should

ask me ___ why I feel sub - lime, I'm ___

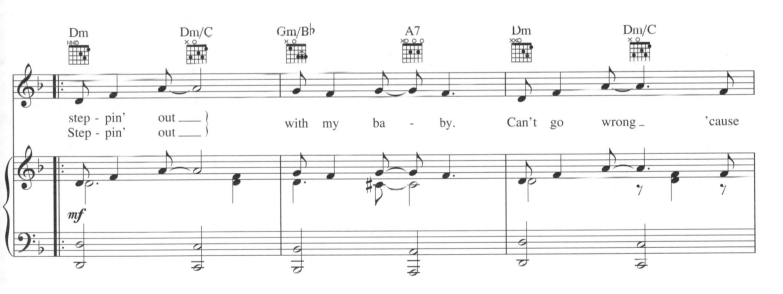

step - pin' out ___ } with my ba - by. Can't go wrong ___ 'cause
Step - pin' out ___ }

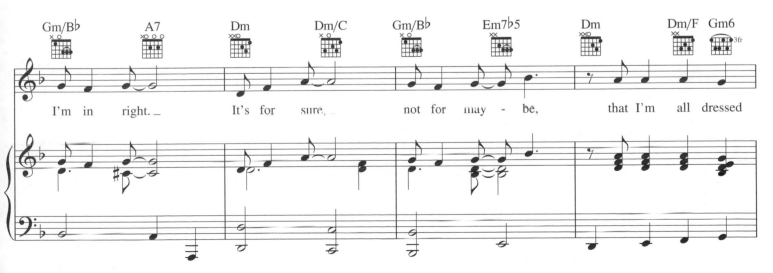

I'm in right. ___ It's for sure, ___ not for may - be, that I'm all dressed

up to - night. __ Step - pin' out ____ with my hon - ey,

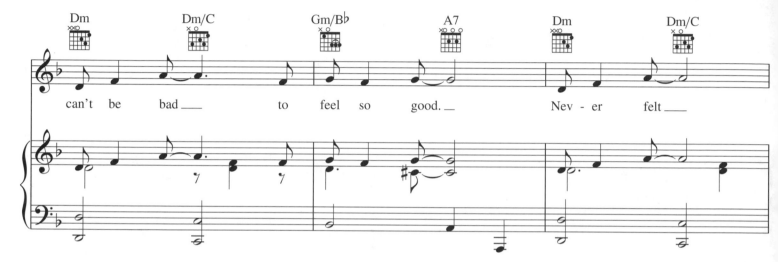

can't be bad ___ to feel so good. __ Nev - er felt ___

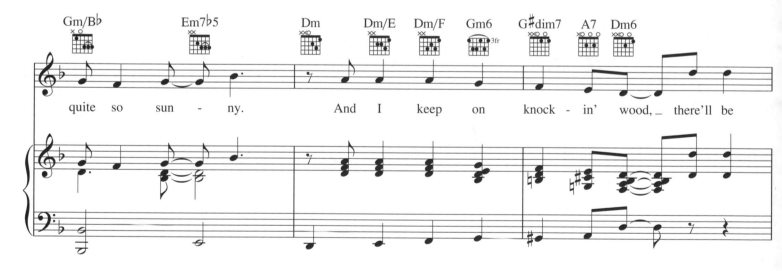

quite so sun - ny. And I keep on knock - in' wood, __ there'll be

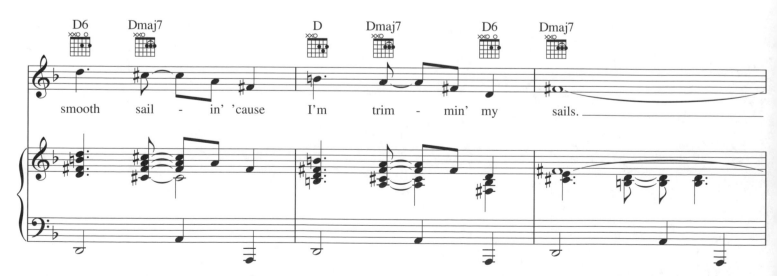

smooth sail - in' 'cause I'm trim - min' my sails. _____

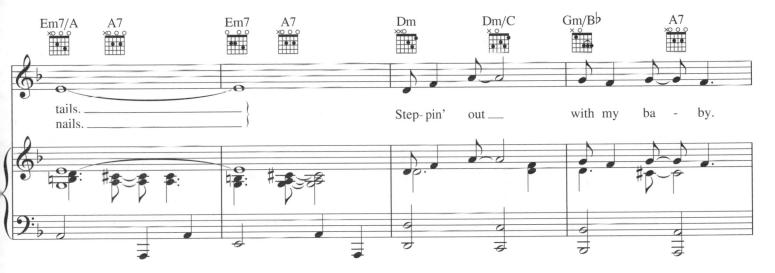

# STOMPIN' AT THE SAVOY

Words by ANDY RAZAF
Music by BENNY GOODMAN,
EDGAR SAMPSON and CHICK WEBB

Sa - voy,_____ the home of sweet ro - mance;___ Sa - voy,__

_____ it wins you at a glance;___ Sa - voy,___ gives hap - py feet a chance___

_____ to dance._____ Your form___

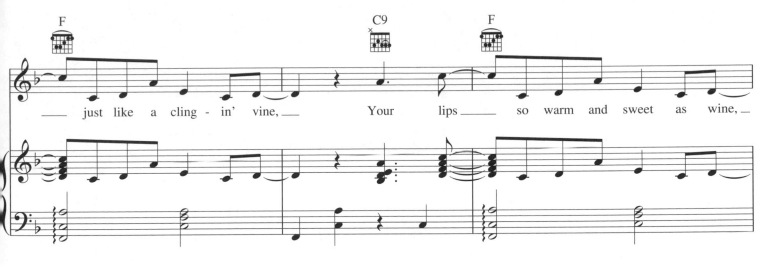

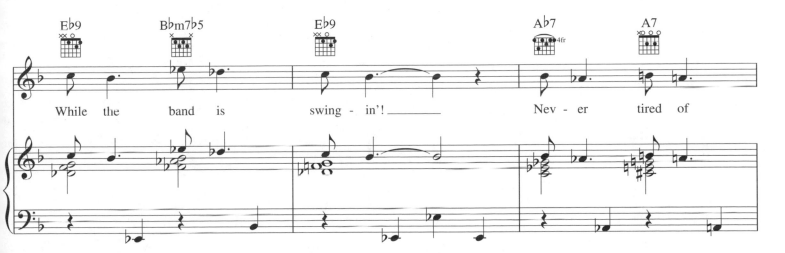

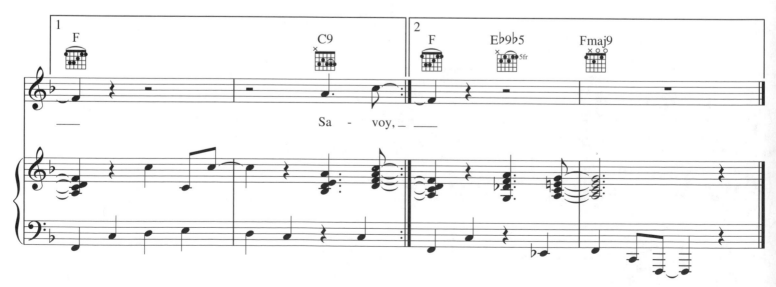

# TEN CENTS A DANCE

## from SIMPLE SIMON

Words by LORENZ HART
Music by RICHARD RODGERS

know; one that the pal - ace fea - tures at ex - act - ly a dime a

**Slowly, quasi rubato**

*poco rit.*

throw. Ten cents a dance, that's what they pay me. Gosh, how they weigh me

down! Ten cents a dance, pan - sies and rough guys,

tough guys who tear my gown! Sev - en to mid - night, I hear drums,

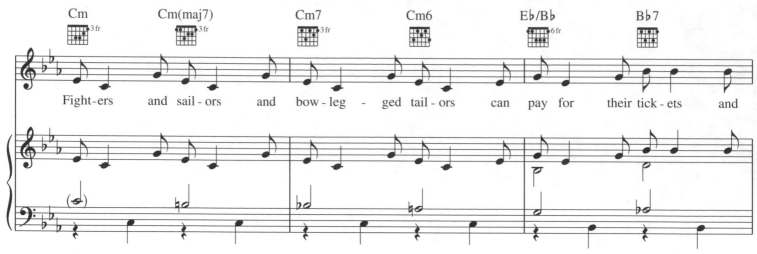

Fight-ers and sail-ors and bow-leg - ged tail-ors can pay for their tick-ets and

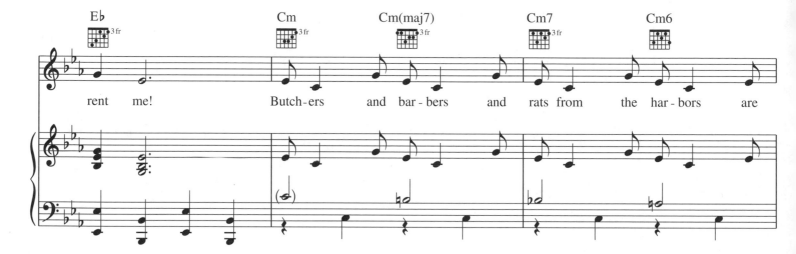

rent me! Butch-ers and bar-bers and rats from the har-bors are

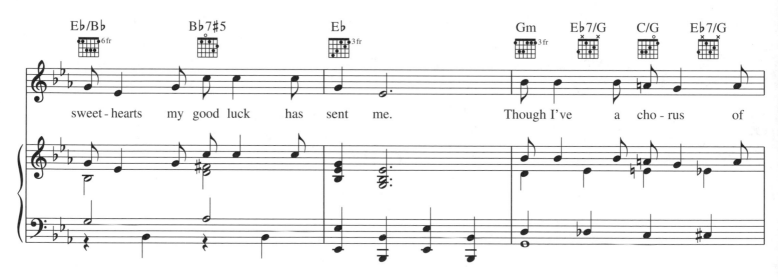

sweet-hearts my good luck has sent me. Though I've a cho-rus of

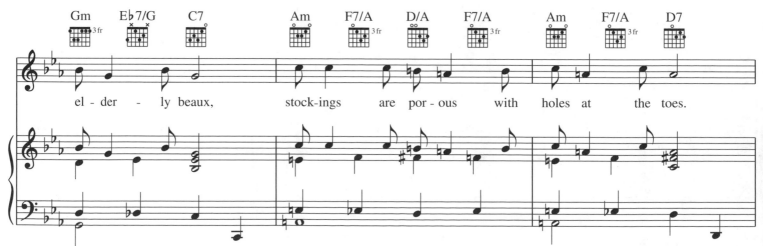

el-der - ly beaux, stock-ings are por-ous with holes at the toes.

# SWEET AND LOVELY

Words and Music by GUS ARNHEIM,
CHARLES N. DANIELS and HARRY TOBIAS

There's sweet-ness in the call of the wood-land dove as his love-song ech-oes through the trees. There's sweet-ness in the rose with its sym-bol of love, float-ing on a sum-mer breeze. But

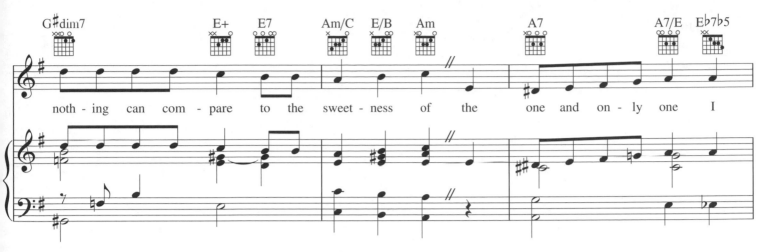

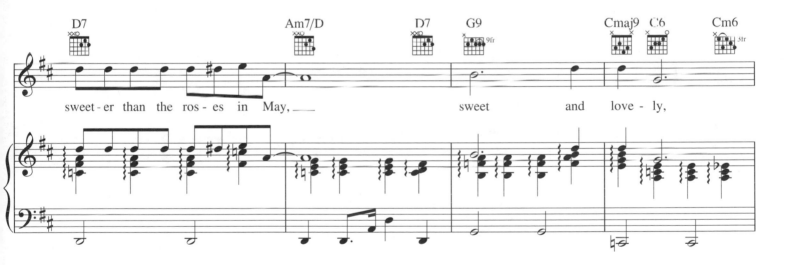
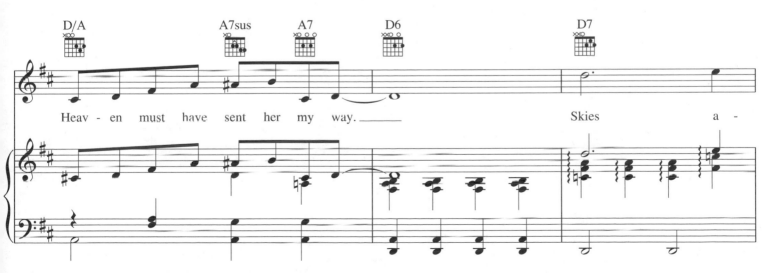

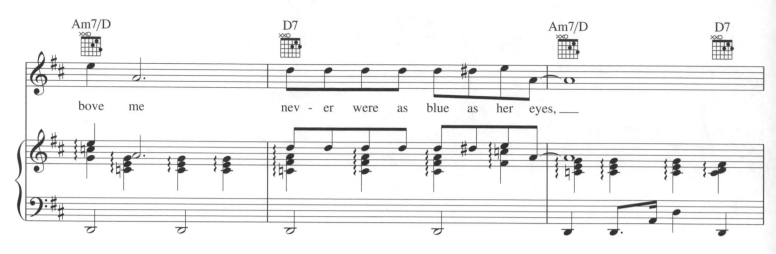

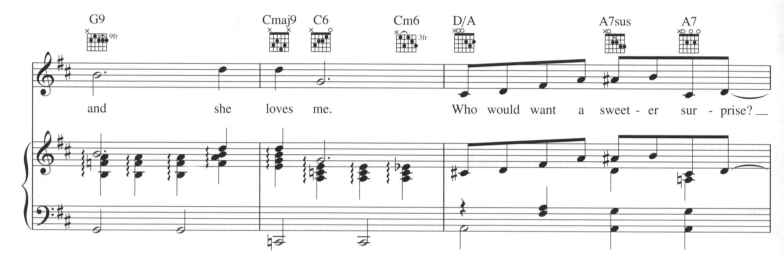

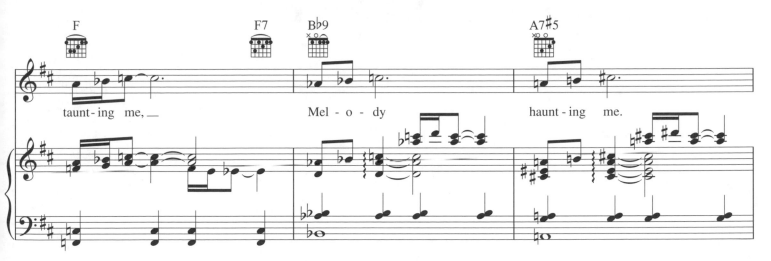

taunt-ing me, __ Mel - o - dy haunt-ing me.

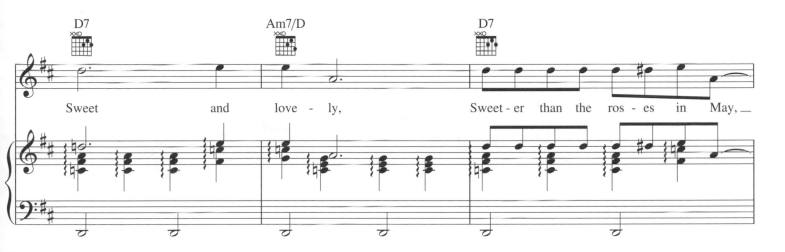

Sweet and love - ly, Sweet - er than the ros - es in May, __

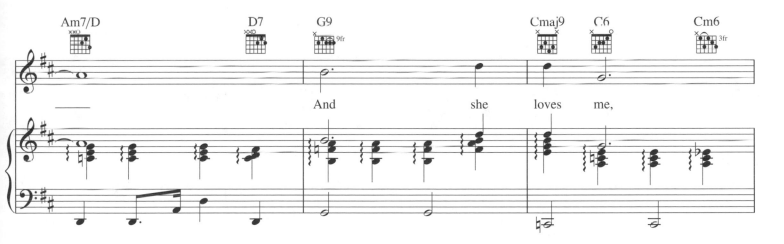

And she loves me,

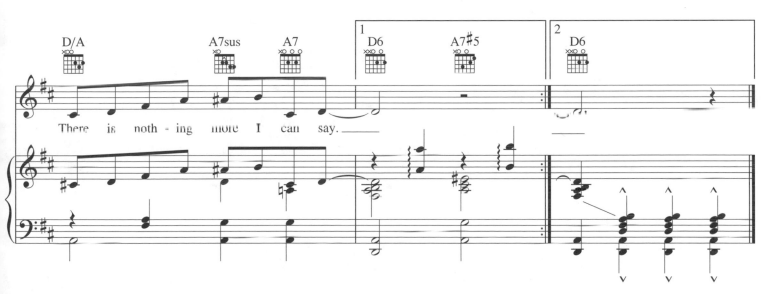

There is noth-ing more I can say. __

# TAKE FIVE

By PAUL DESMOND

**Up-tempo Swing**

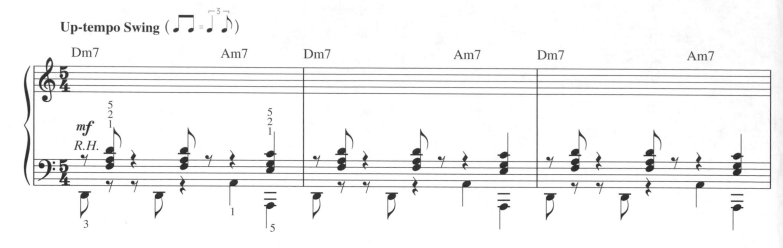

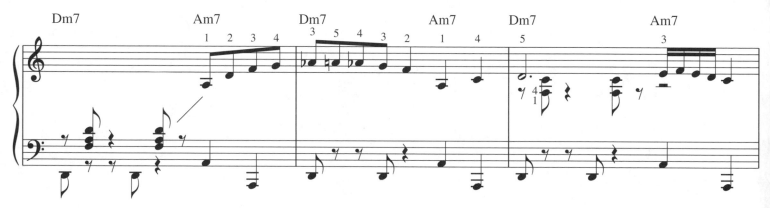

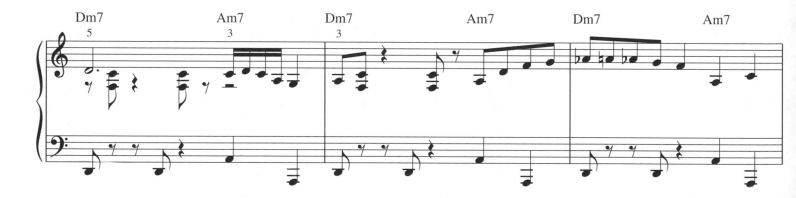

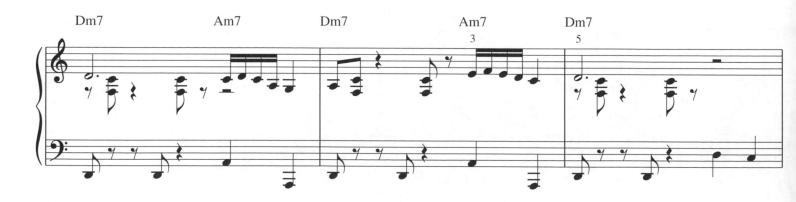

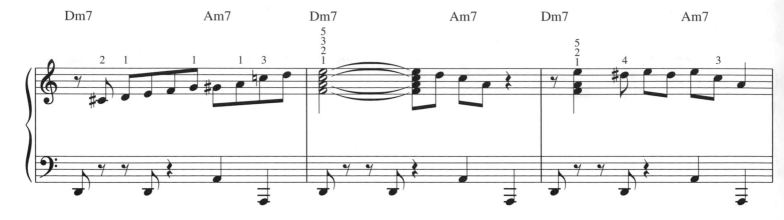

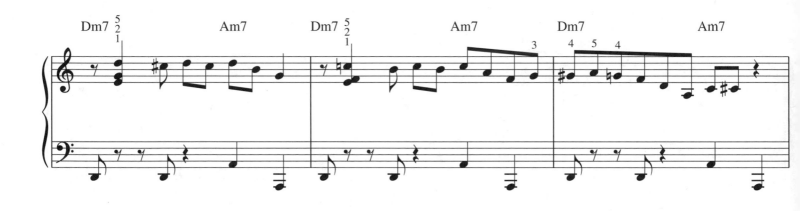

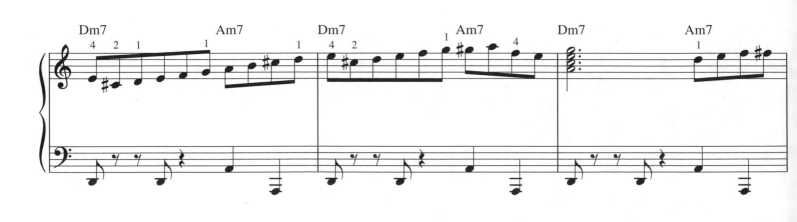

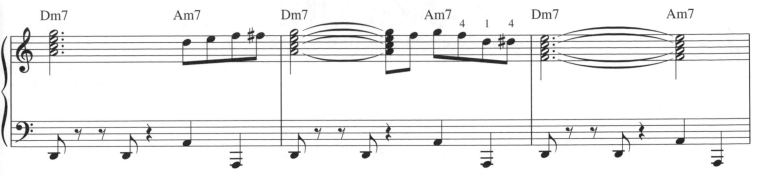

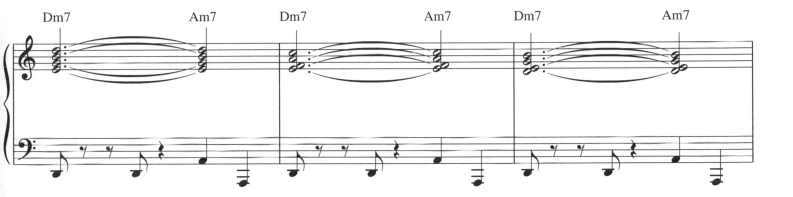

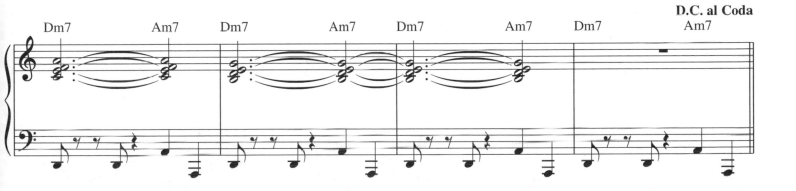

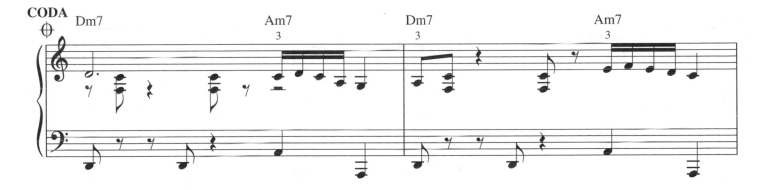

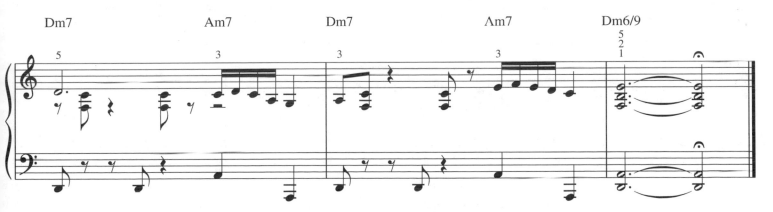

# TANGERINE
## from the Paramount Picture THE FLEET'S IN

Words by JOHNNY MERCER
Music by VICTOR SCHERTZINGER

**Moderately, with expression**

South A-mer-i-can sto-ries _____ tell of a girl who's

quite a dream, ___ the beau-ty of her race. Though you doubt all the

sto-ries _____ and think the tales are just a bit ex-

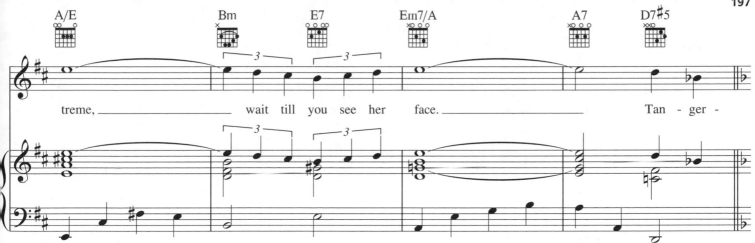

treme, _____ wait till you see her face. _____ Tan - ger -

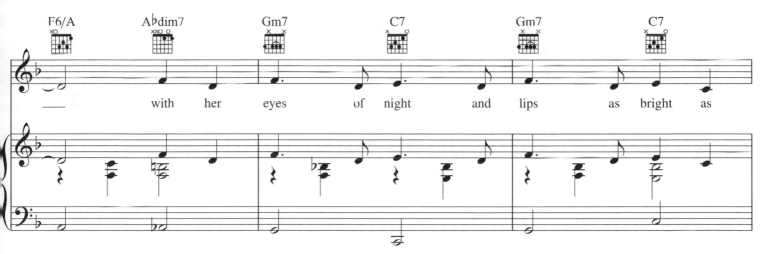

ine, _____ she is all they claim, _____

___ with her eyes of night and lips as bright as

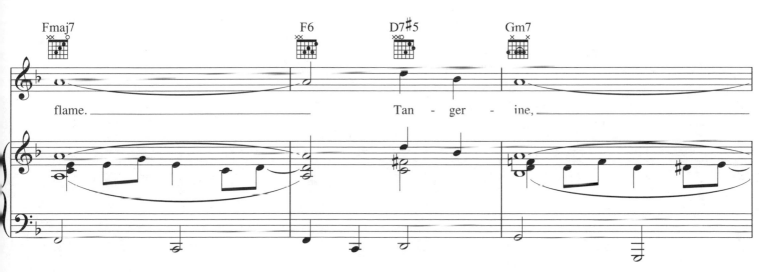

flame. _____ Tan - ger - ine, _____

when she danc - es by, _____ se - ño -

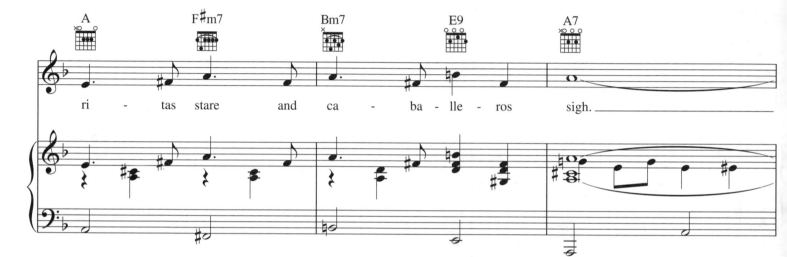

ri - tas stare and ca - ba - lle - ros sigh. _____

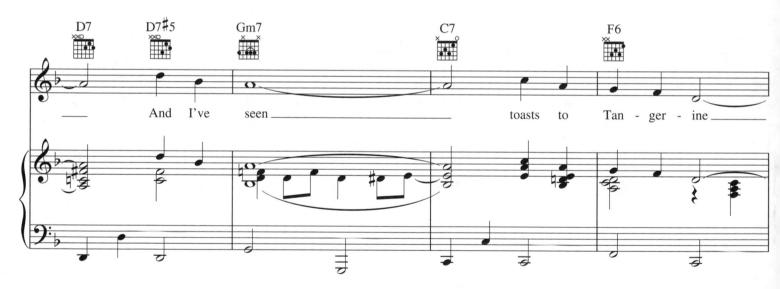

\_\_ And I've seen _____ toasts to Tan - ger - ine \_\_\_\_

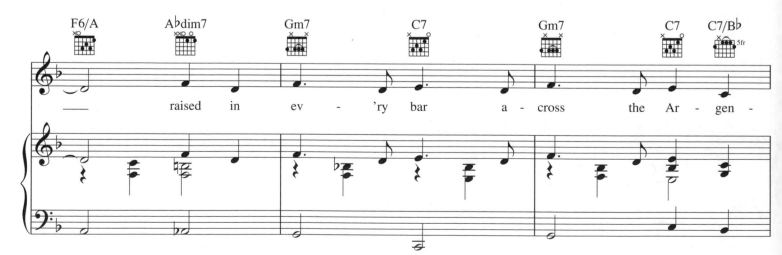

\_\_ raised in ev - 'ry bar a - cross the Ar - gen -

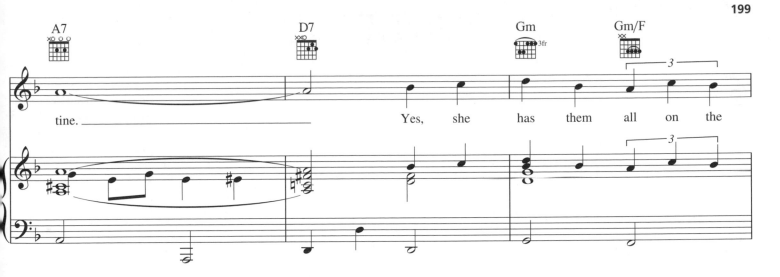

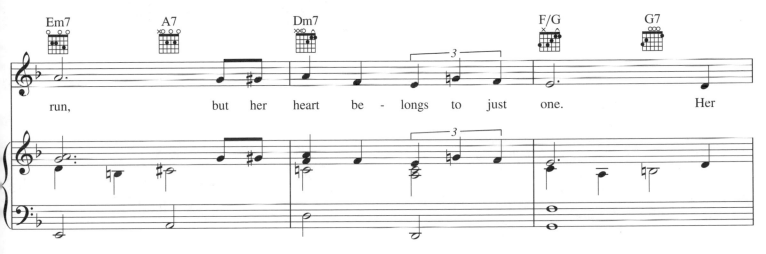

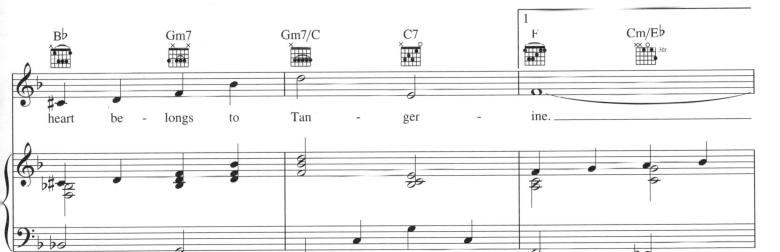

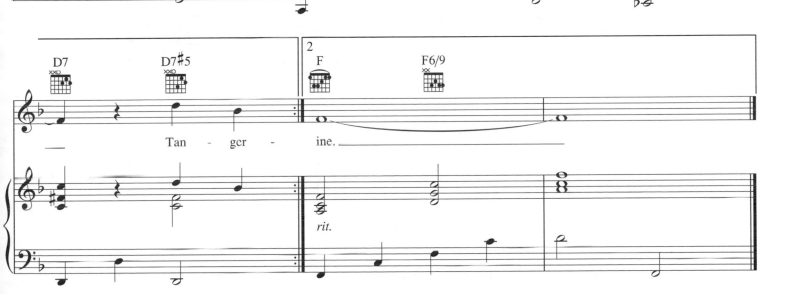

# TENDERLY
## from TORCH SONG

Lyric by JACK LAWRENCE
Music by WALTER GROSS

**Moderately**

The eve-ning breeze ca-ressed the trees ten-der - ly; _____

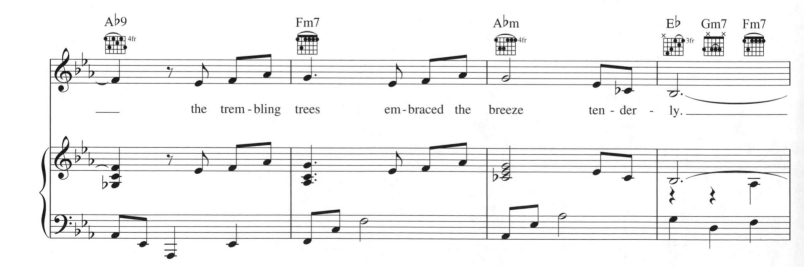

_____ the trem-bling trees em-braced the breeze ten-der - ly. _____

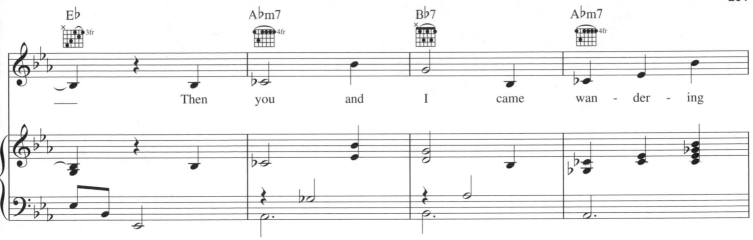

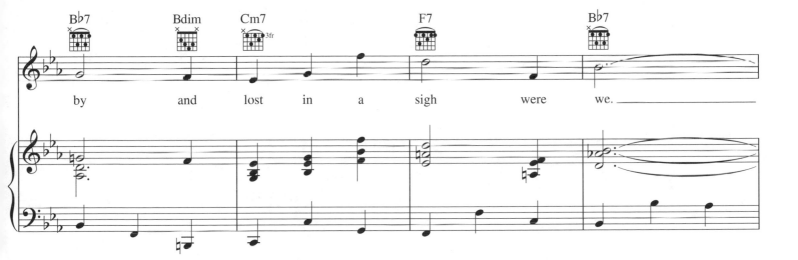

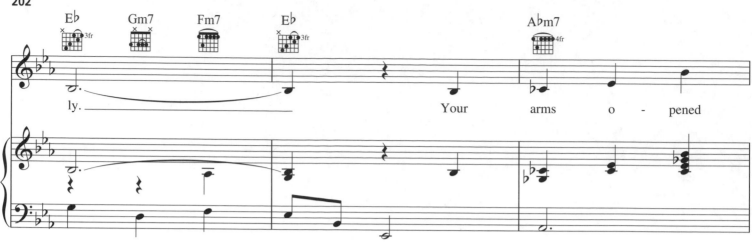

ly. _____ Your arms o - pened

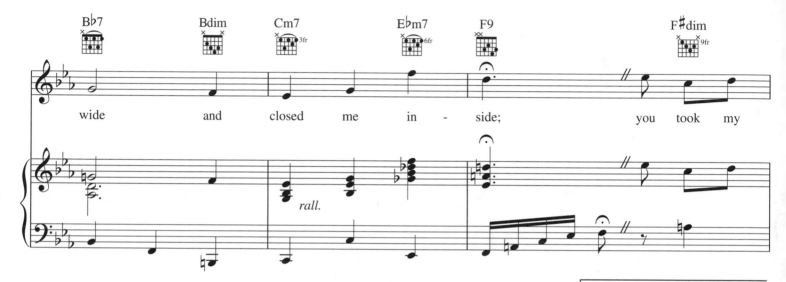

wide and closed me in - side; you took my

lips, you took my love so ten - der - ly.

The eve - ning ly. _____

# THAT OLD BLACK MAGIC

from the Paramount Picture STAR SPANGLED RHYTHM

Words by JOHNNY MERCER
Music by HAROLD ARLEN

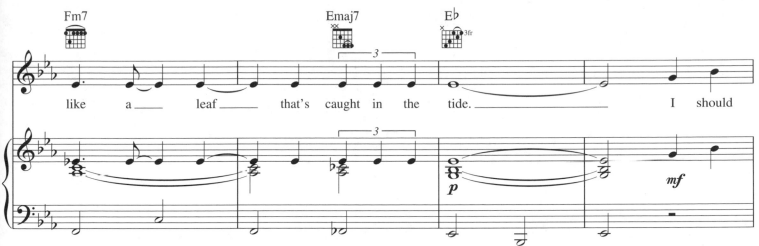

like a \_\_\_ leaf \_\_\_ that's caught in the tide. _____ I should

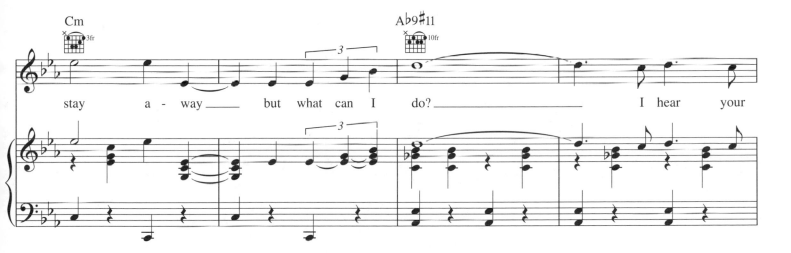

stay a - way \_\_\_ but what can I do? _____ I hear your

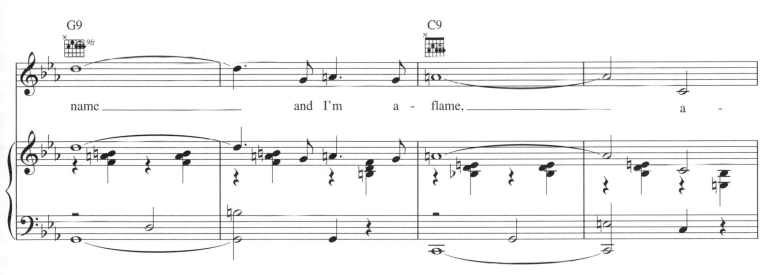

name _____ and I'm a - flame, _____ a -

flame with such \_\_\_ a burn-ing de - sire _____ that on - ly your

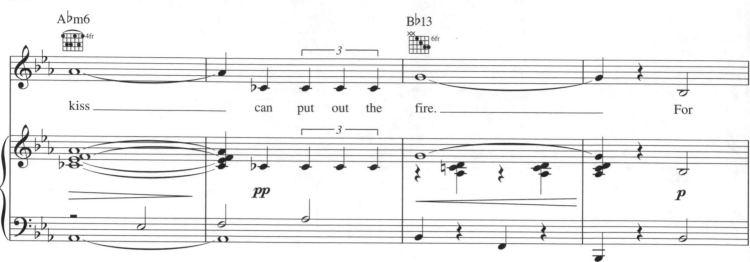

kiss _____ can put out the fire. _____ For

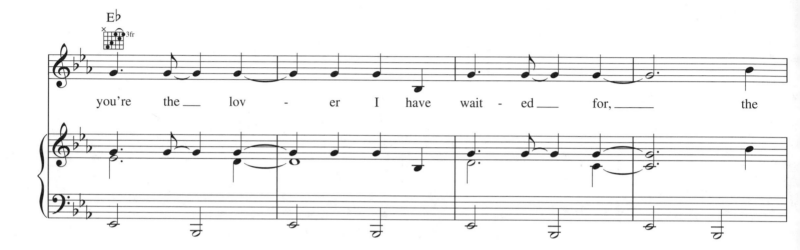

you're the __ lov - er I have wait - ed __ for, __ the

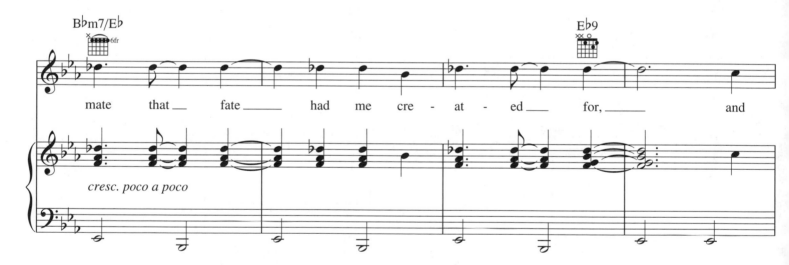

mate that __ fate __ had me cre - at - ed __ for, __ and

ev - 'ry __ time __ your lips meet mine, _____ dar - ling,

# THERE IS NO GREATER LOVE

Words by MARTY SYMES
Music by ISHAM JONES

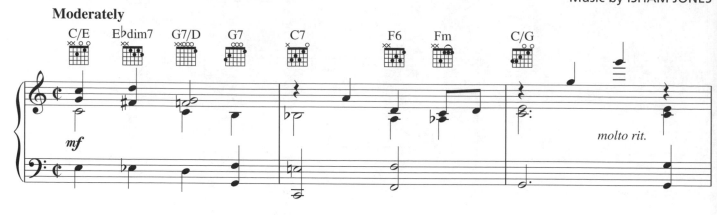

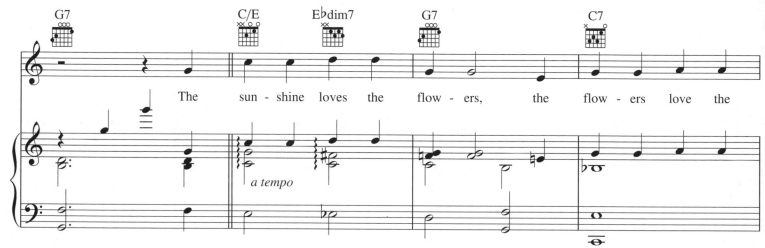

The sun-shine loves the flow-ers, the flow-ers love the

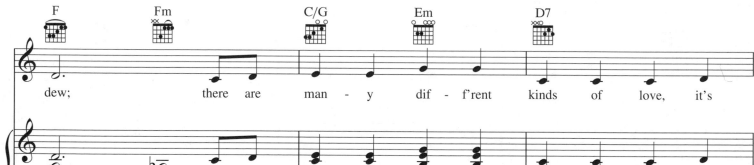

dew; there are man-y dif-f'rent kinds of love, it's

true.

The stars all love the

# THERE'LL BE SOME CHANGES MADE

from ALL THAT JAZZ

Words by BILLY HIGGINS
Music by W. BENTON OVERSTREET

For there's a change in the weath - er, there's a change in the sea, ___

so from now on there'll be a change in me. ___ My walk will be dif - f'rent, my

# THEY SAY IT'S WONDERFUL

## from the Stage Production ANNIE GET YOUR GUN

Words and Music by
IRVING BERLIN

set my heart a - glow.
heard is real - ly so.

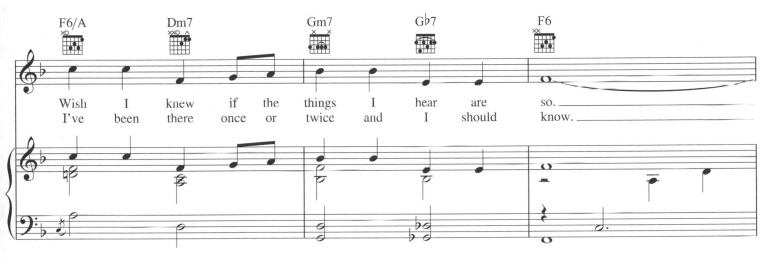

Wish I knew if the things I hear are so.
I've been there once or twice and I should know.

**Slowly**

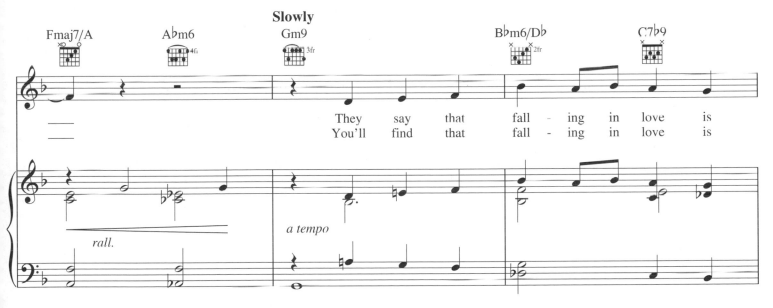

They say that fall - ing in love is
You'll find that fall - ing in love is

*rall.*     *a tempo*

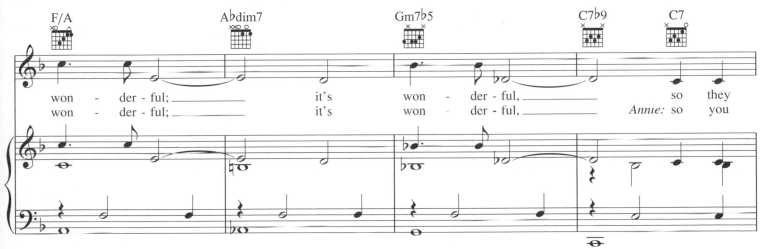

won - der - ful; _____ it's won - der - ful, _____ so they
won - der - ful; _____ it's won - der - ful, _____ *Annie:* so you

tell me that love is grand, and the thing that's
shout - ing that love is grand, and to hold a

known as ro - mance is won - der - ful, won - der - ful
man in your arms is won - der - ful, won - der - ful

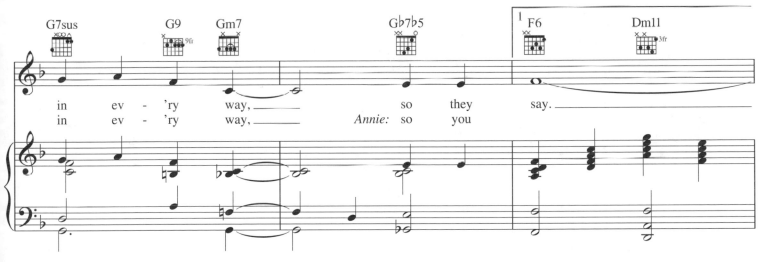

in ev - 'ry way, _____ so they say. _____
in ev - 'ry way, _____ *Annie:* so you

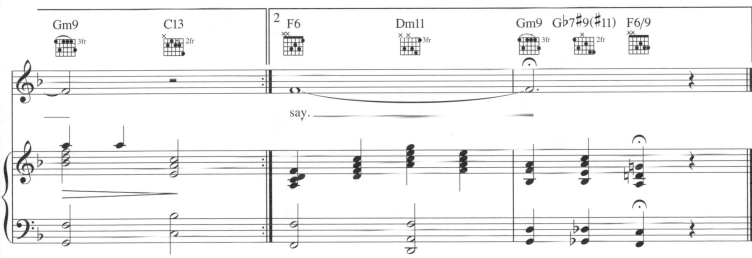

say. _____

# TOO LATE NOW

from ROYAL WEDDING

Words by ALAN JAY LERNER
Music by BURTON LANE

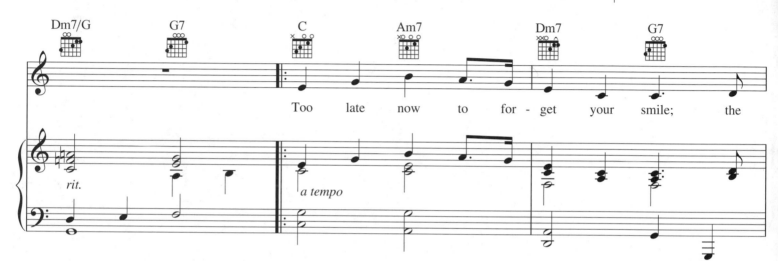

Too late now to for-get your smile; the

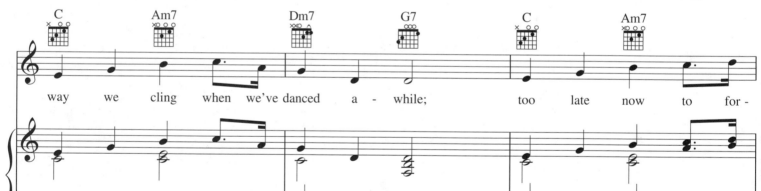

way we cling when we've danced a - while; too late now to for-

get and go on to some - one new.

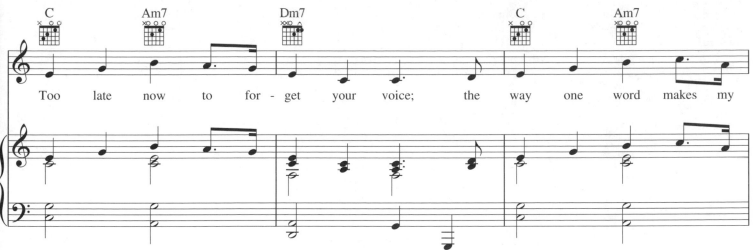

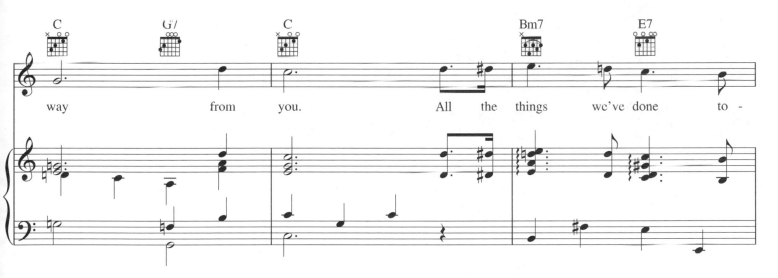

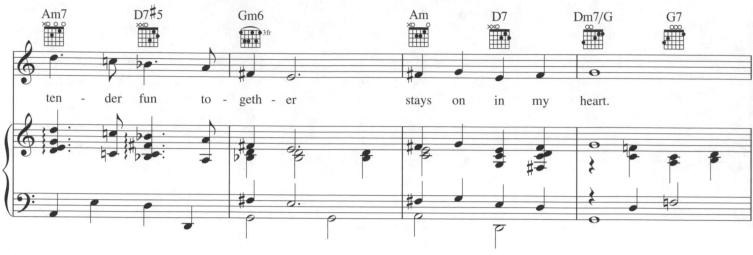

ten - der fun to - geth - er stays on in my heart.

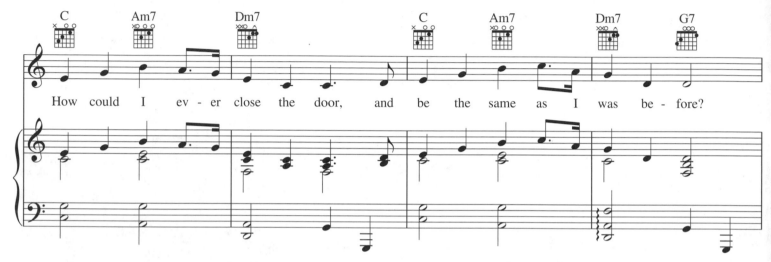

How could I ev - er close the door, and be the same as I was be - fore?

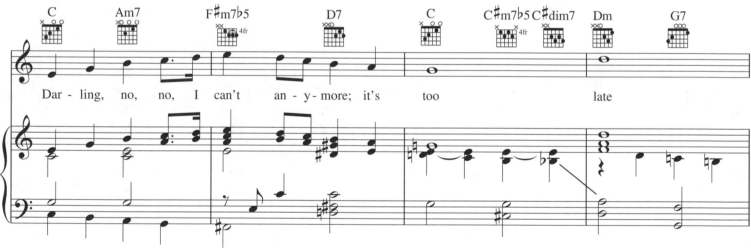

Dar - ling, no, no, I can't an - y - more; it's too late

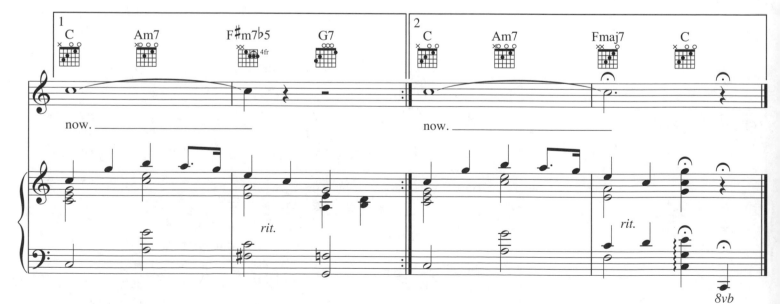

now. _____ now. _____

*8vb*

# WE'VE ONLY JUST BEGUN

Words and Music by ROGER NICHOLS
and PAUL WILLIAMS

We've on-ly just be-gun _____ to live. _____

White lace and prom - is - es, a kiss for luck _ and we're

on our way. _____

(1.) Be - fore the ris - ing
(2., D.S.) And when the eve - ning

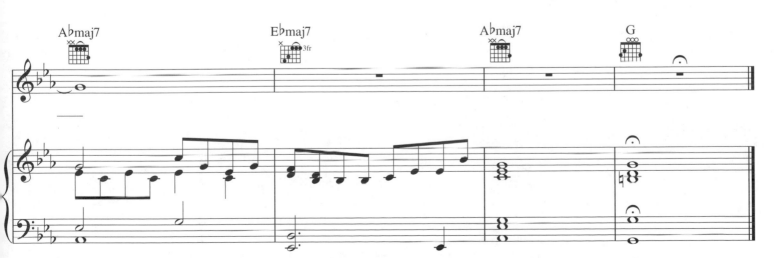

# TWO SLEEPY PEOPLE

from the Paramount Motion Picture THANKS FOR THE MEMORY

Words by FRANK LOESSER
Music by HOAGY CARMICHAEL

Tick, tock! Cuck - oo! Here we are, out of cig - a - rettes, \_
Here we are, in the co - zy chair, \_

hold - ing hands and yawn - ing, look how late it gets. \_\_\_
pick - ing on a wish - bone from the Frig - i - daire. \_\_\_

Two sleep - y peo - ple by dawn's ear - ly light, and
Two sleep - y peo - ple with noth - ing to say, and

too much in love to say "Good - night."

rent this lit - tle    nest, ___    and  get   a   bit   of   rest.    Well,

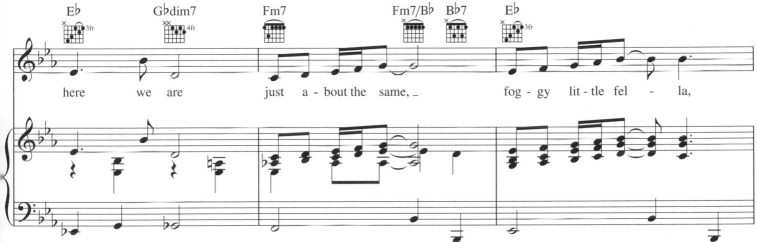

here   we   are    just  a - bout the  same, _    fog - gy  lit - tle  fel - la,

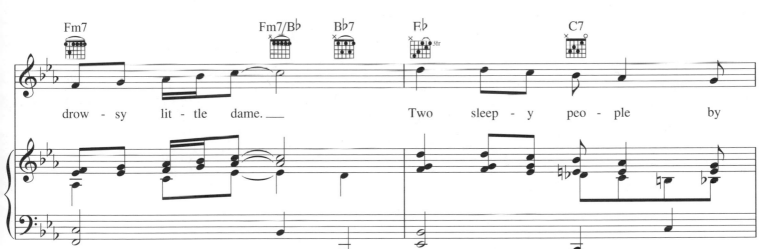

drow - sy  lit - tle  dame. ___    Two    sleep - y   peo - ple   by

dawn's  ear - ly  light,    and   too  much  in  love  to  say  "Good - night."

# UNTIL IT'S TIME FOR YOU TO GO
## from ELVIS ON TOUR

Words and Music by
BUFFY SAINTE-MARIE

and here we'll stay    un-til it's time    for you to
and here you'll stay    un-til it's time    for you to

go.                    Yes, we're    go _____

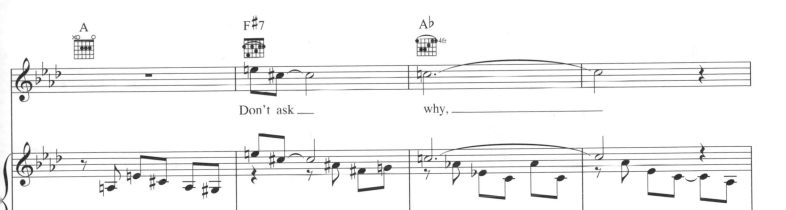

Don't ask ___    why, _____

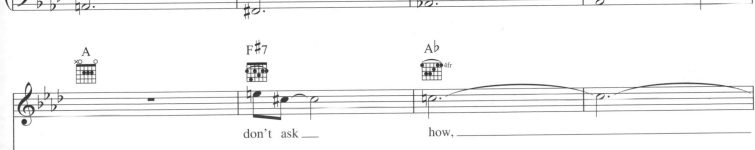

don't ask ___    how, _____

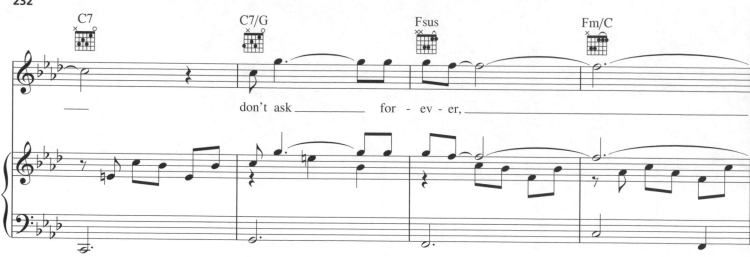

don't ask _____ for - ev - er, _____

love me ____ now. _____ This love of

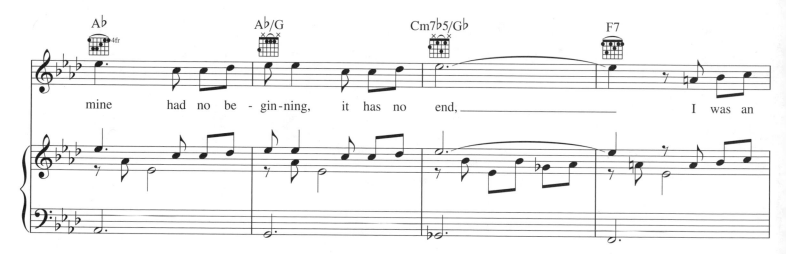

mine had no be - gin - ning, it has no end, _____ I was an

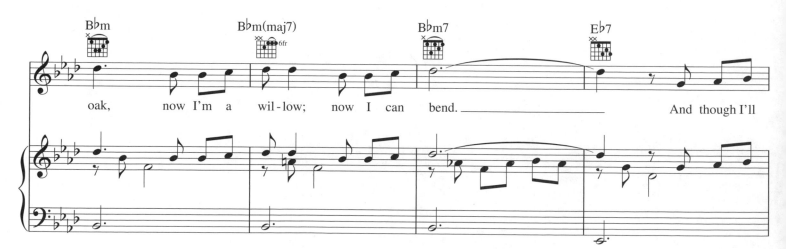

oak, now I'm a wil - low; now I can bend. _____ And though I'll

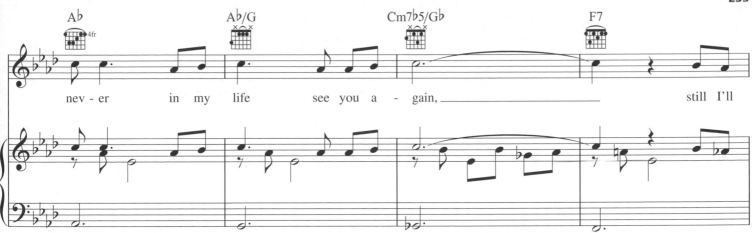

nev - er  in  my  life  see you a - gain,_____  still I'll

stay  un - til  it's  time  for  you  to  go._____

Don't ask ___  why  of  me,

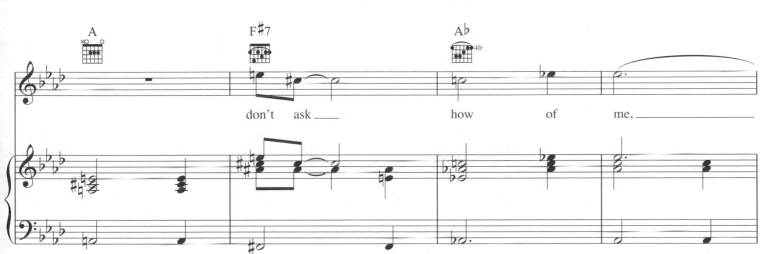

don't ask ___  how  of  me,_____

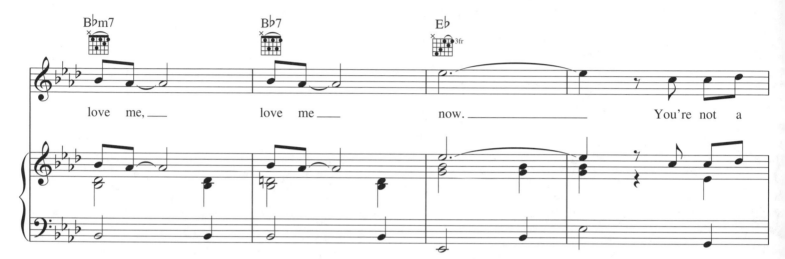

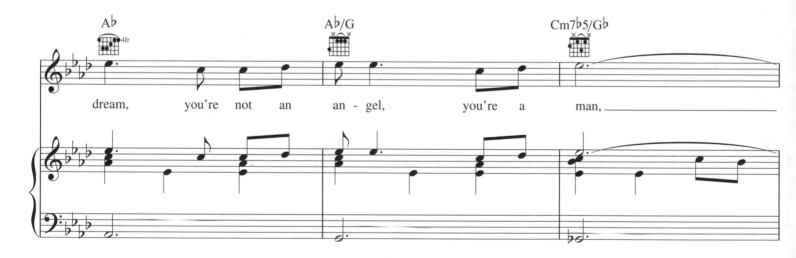

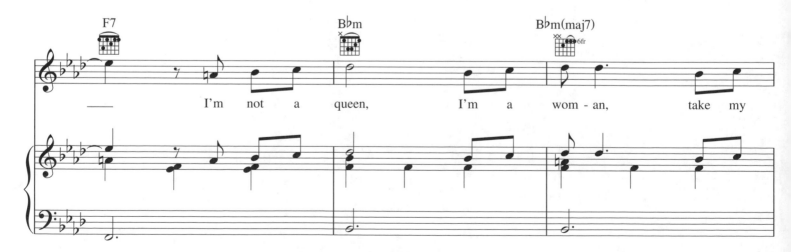

hand. _____ We'll make a space in the

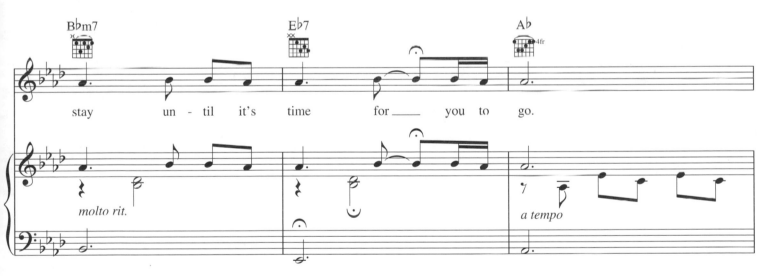

lives that we'd planned, _____ and here we'll

stay un- til it's time for ___ you to go.

*molto rit.* *a tempo*

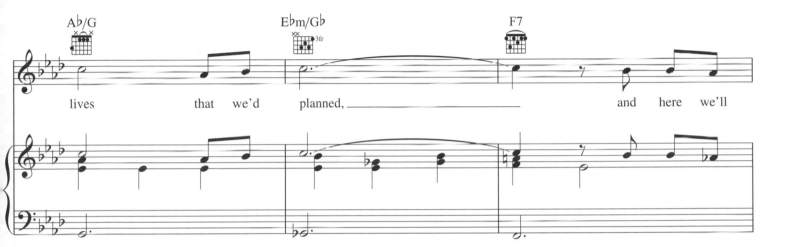

# WHAT A DIFF'RENCE A DAY MADE

English Words by STANLEY ADAMS
Music and Spanish Words by MARIA GREVER

# WHAT'S NEW?

Words by JOHNNY BURKE
Music by BOB HAGGART

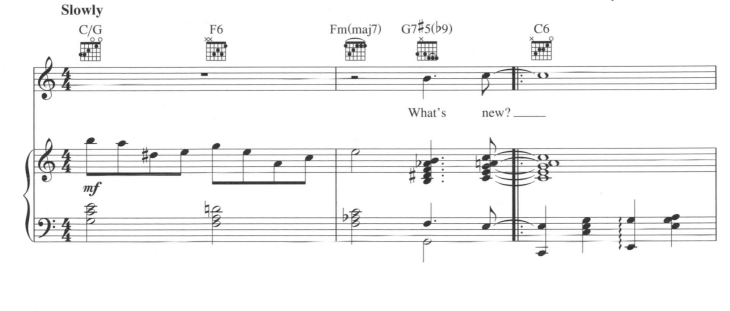

What's new? _____

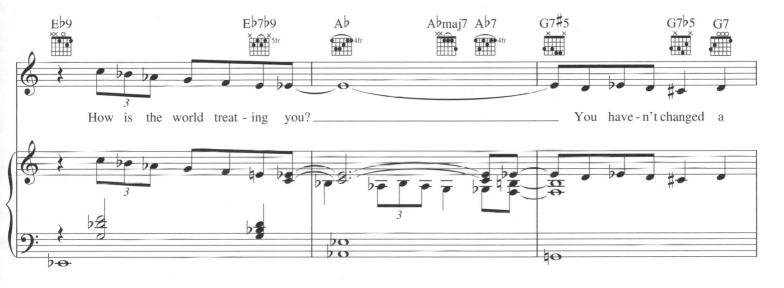

How is the world treat-ing you? _____ You have-n't changed a

bit; love-ly as ev-er, I must ad-mit. _____

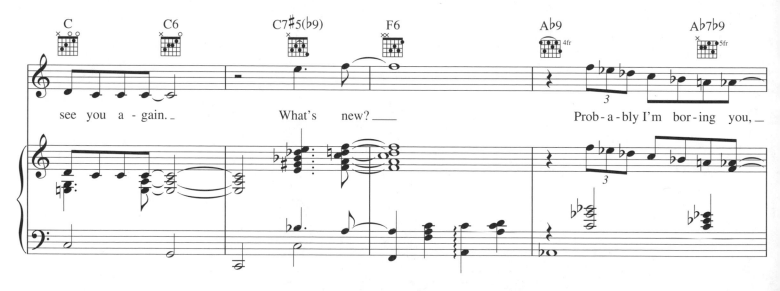

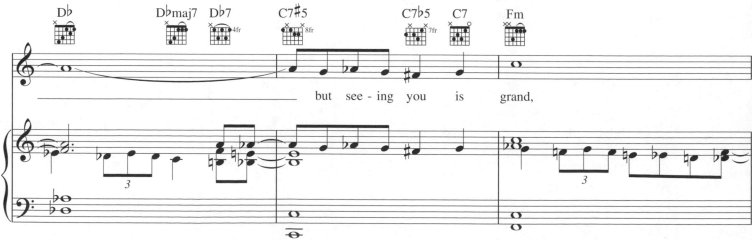

# WHAT'LL I DO?
## from MUSIC BOX REVUE OF 1924

Words and Music by
IRVING BERLIN

Gone is the ro - mance that was so di - vine. ___ 'Tis bro - ken and can - not be mend - ed. You must go

Do you re - mem - ber a night so filled with bliss? ___ The moon - light was soft - ly de - scend - ing. Your lips and

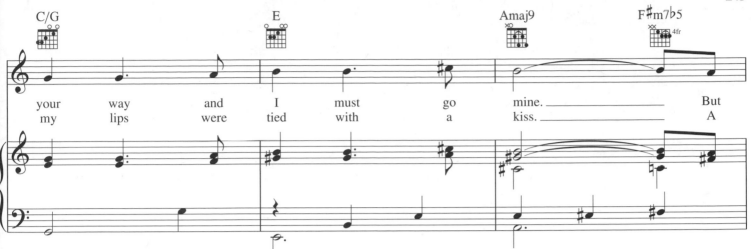

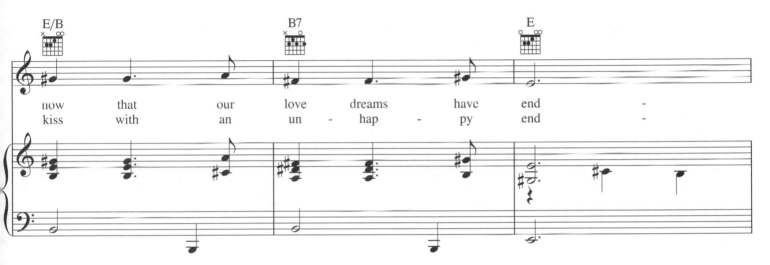

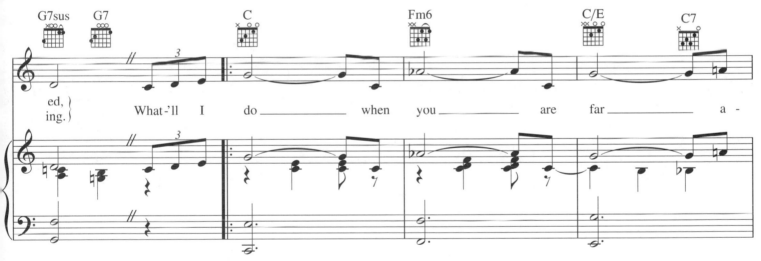

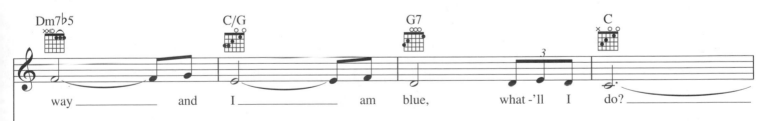

What-'ll I do _____ when I _____ am won - d'ring

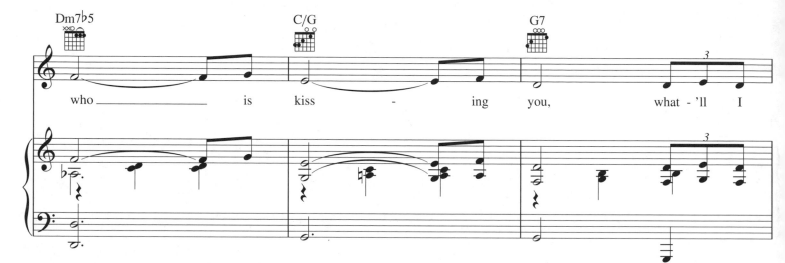

who _____ is kiss - ing you, what -'ll I

do? _____ What -'ll I do _____ with

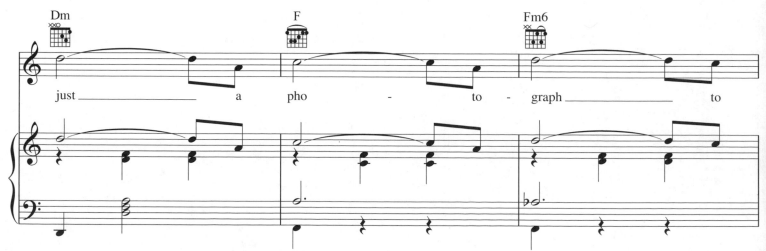

just _____ a pho - to - graph _____ to

# WHEN SUNNY GETS BLUE

Lyric by JACK SEGAL
Music by MARVIN FISHER

**Slow Blues tempo**

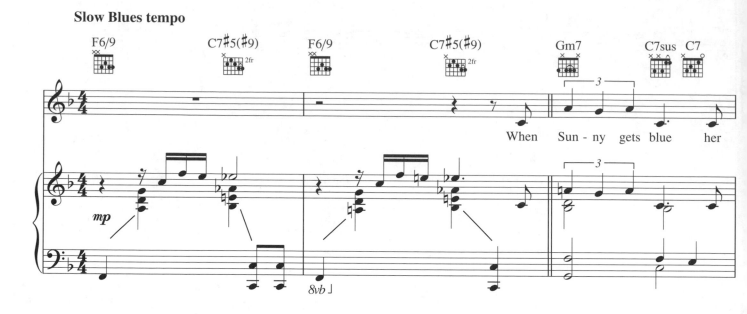

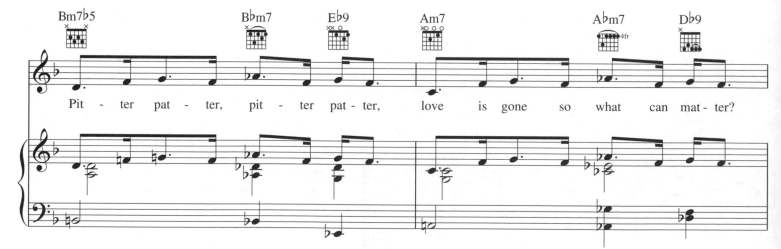

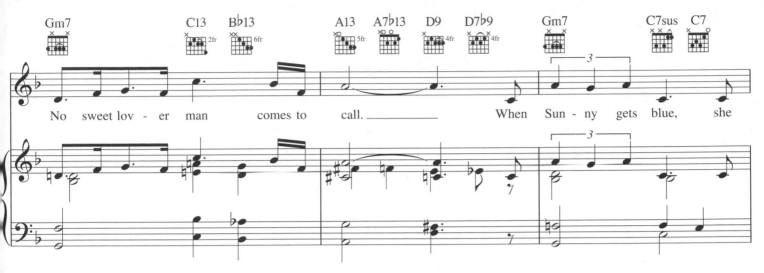

No sweet lov - er man comes to call. ____ When Sun - ny gets blue, she

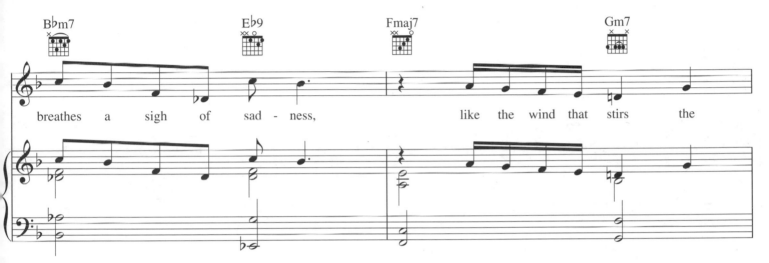

breathes a sigh of sad - ness, like the wind that stirs the

trees. Wind that sets the leaves to sway - in',

like some vi - o - lins are play - in' weird and haunt - ing mel - o -

# WHY DON'T YOU DO RIGHT
## (Get Me Some Money, Too!)

By JOE McCOY

**Slow Blues tempo**

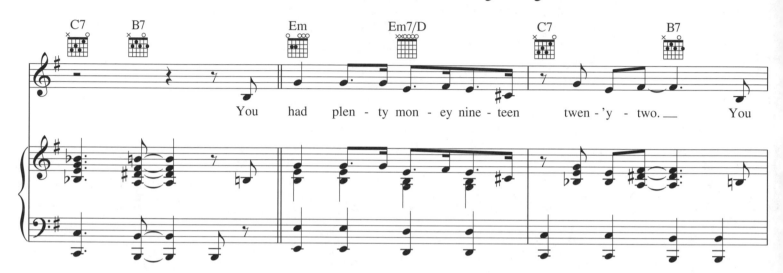

You had plen-ty mon-ey nine-teen twen-'y-two. ___ You

let oth-er peo-ple make a fool of you. ___ Why don't you do right, ___

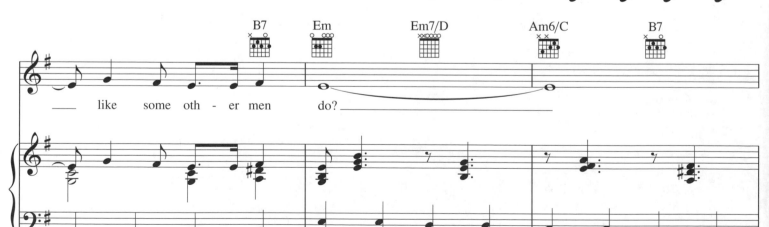

___ like some oth-er men do? ___

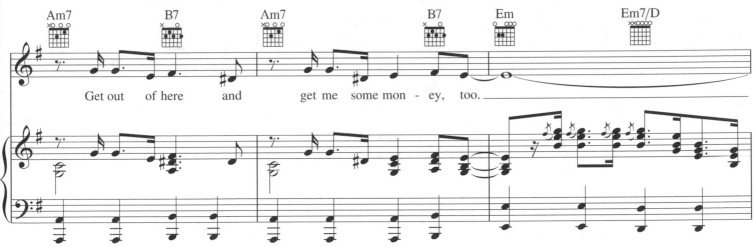

Get out of here and get me some mon - ey, too. _____

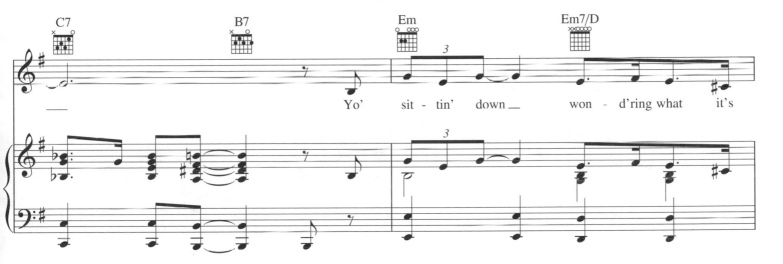

_____ Yo' sit - tin' down ___ won - d'ring what it's

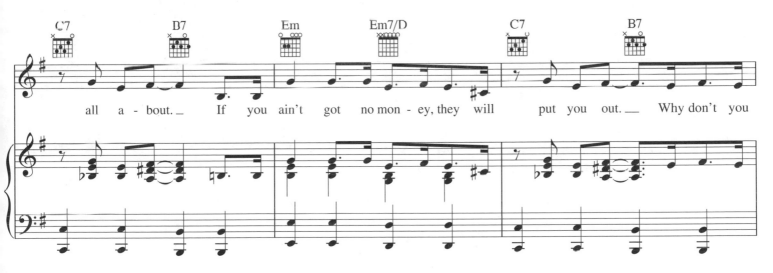

all a - bout. __ If you ain't got no mon - ey, they will put you out. __ Why don't you

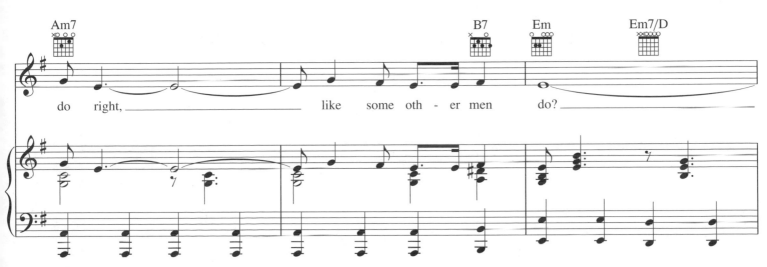

do right, _____ like some oth - er men do? _____

Get out of here and get me some mon - ey, too.

If

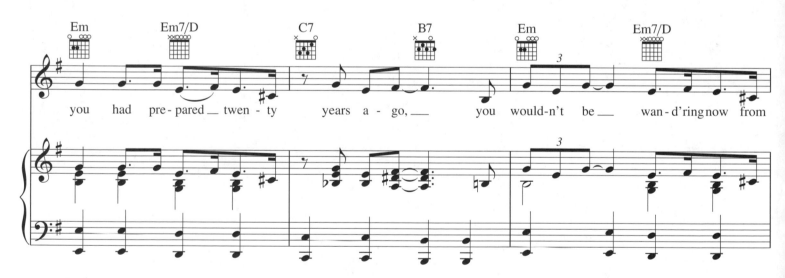

you had pre - pared __ twen - ty years a - go, __ you would-n't be __ wan - d'ring now from

do' to do'. __ Why don't you do right, _____ like some oth - er men

# WILLOW WEEP FOR ME

Words and Music by
ANN RONELL

love - ly sum-mer dream, _ Gone and left me here _ to keep my tears ___ in - to the stream, _

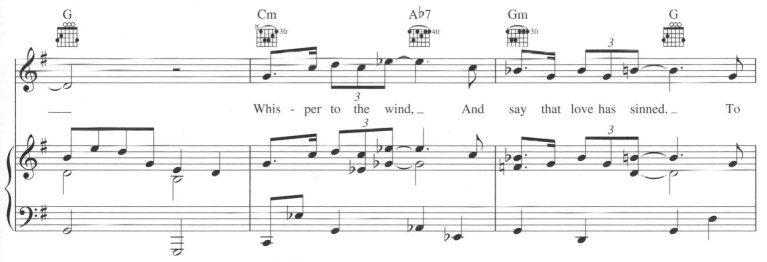

Sad as I can be, hear me wil - low and weep for me. _____

_ Whis - per to the wind, _ And say that love has sinned. _ To

leave my heart a - break - ing and mak - ing a moan. _ Mur - mur to the night _ to

# WITCHCRAFT

Music by CY COLEMAN
Lyric by CAROLYN LEIGH

Shades of old Lu - cre - tia Bor - gia! There's a dev - il in you to - night, __ 'n' al - though my heart a - dores __ ya, my head says __ it ain't right, __ right to let you

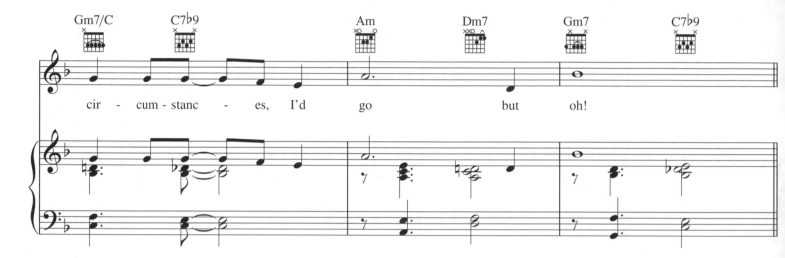

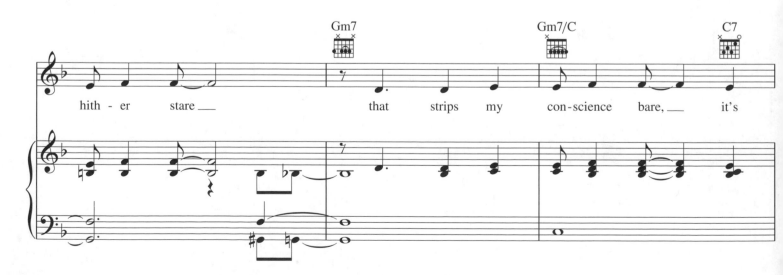

witch - craft. _____ And I've got

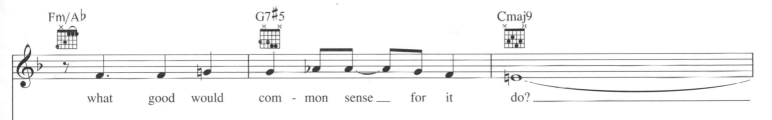

no de - fense _ for it, the heat is too in - tense _ for it,

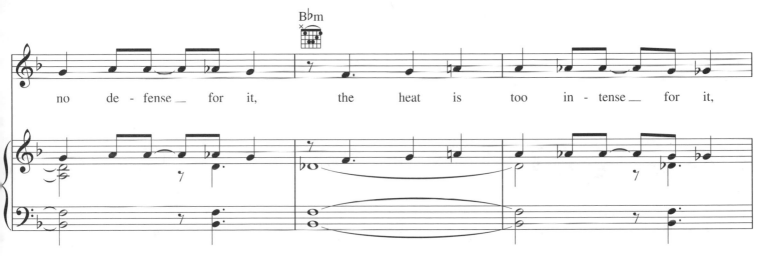

what good would com - mon sense _ for it do? _____

_____ 'Cause _ it's witch - craft! _ Wick - ed

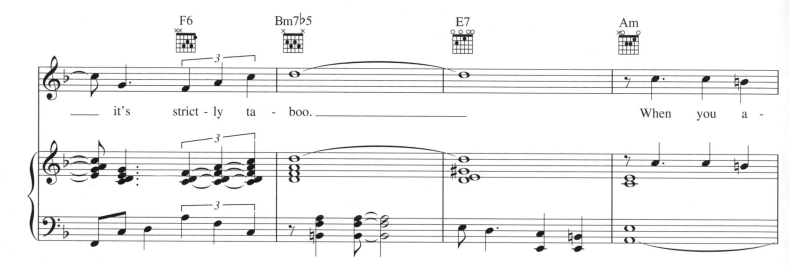

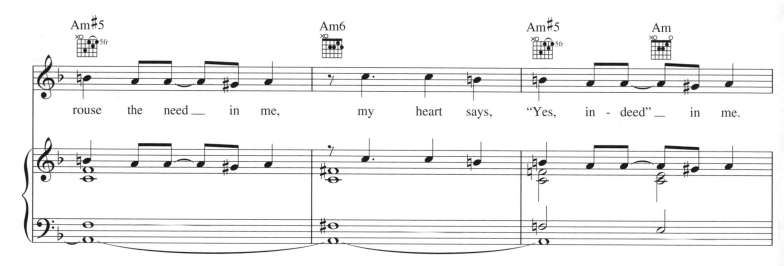

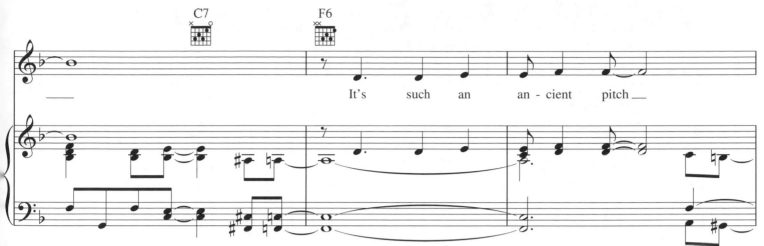

It's such an an-cient pitch __

but onc I would-n't switch __ 'cause there's no

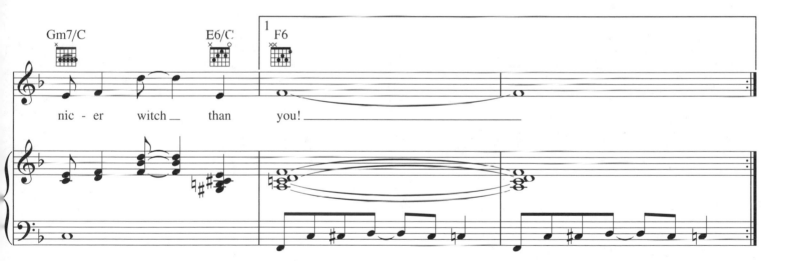

nic - er witch __ than you! _____

you! _____

# WITH A SONG IN MY HEART

## from SPRING IS HERE

Words by LORENZ HART
Music by RICHARD RODGERS

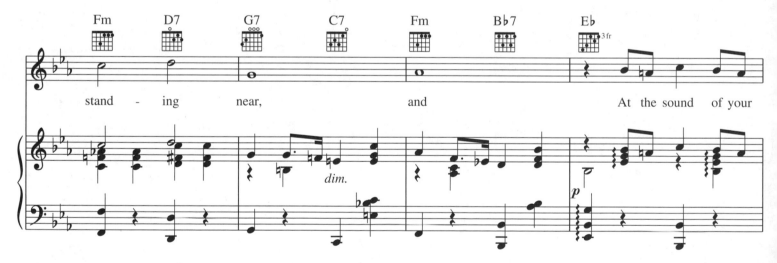

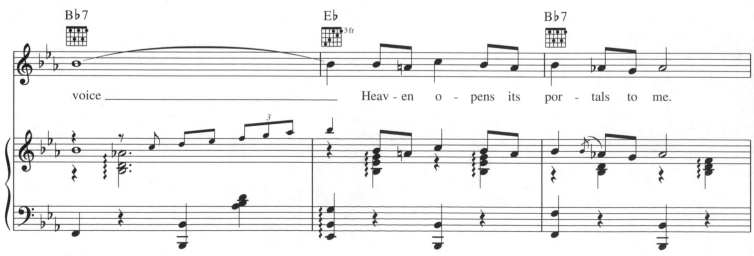

# WIVES AND LOVERS
## (Hey, Little Girl)
### from the Paramount Picture WIVES AND LOVERS

Words by HAL DAVID
Music by BURT BACHARACH

arms ____ the mo - ment he ____ comes home to you. { I'm
                                                    { He's

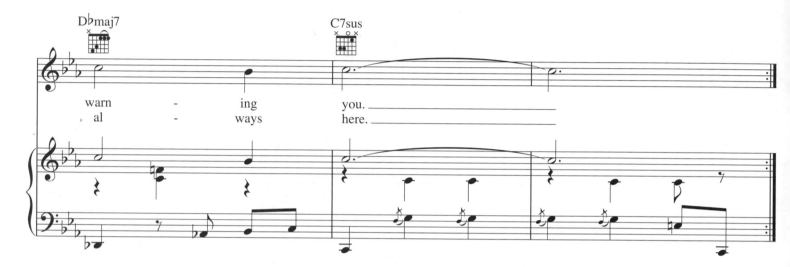

warn - ing you. _____
al - ways here. _____

Hey, lit - tle girl, bet - ter wear some - thing pret - ty,

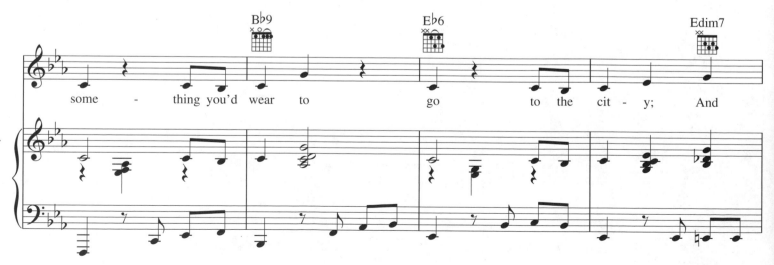

some - thing you'd wear to go to the cit - y; And

dim all the lights, pour the wine, start the mu - sic,

time to get read - y for love. _____ Oh,

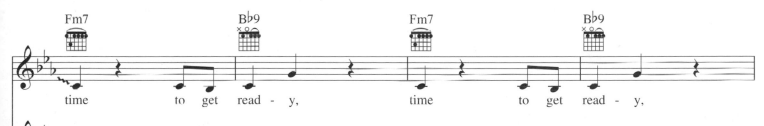

time to get read - y, time to get read - y,

time to get read - y for love. _____

*8vb* ⌡

# YESTERDAY ONCE MORE

Words and Music by JOHN BETTIS
and RICHARD CARPENTER

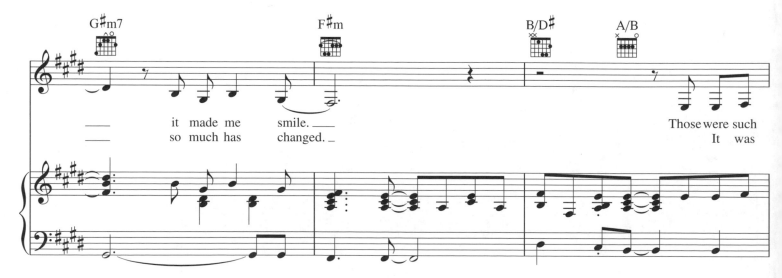

hap - py times, _ and not so long a - go, _ how I won - dered where they'd gone. _
songs of love _ that I would sing to then, _ and I'd mem - o - rize each word. _

But they're back a - gain, _ just like a long lost friend, _ all the
Those old mel - o - dies _ still sound so good to me _ as they

*building*

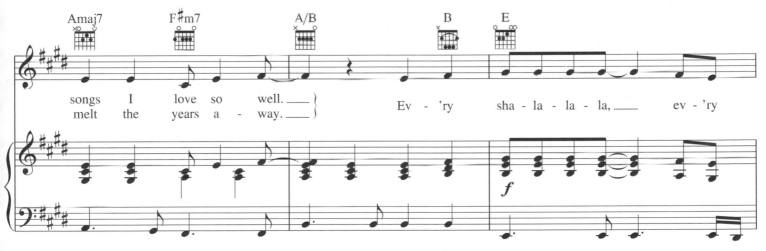

songs I love so well. _
melt the years a - way. _

Ev - 'ry sha - la - la - la, _ ev - 'ry

*f*

whoa _ whoa _ still shines. _

Ev - 'ry

shing - a - ling - a - ling that they're start - ing to sing's _ so fine. _

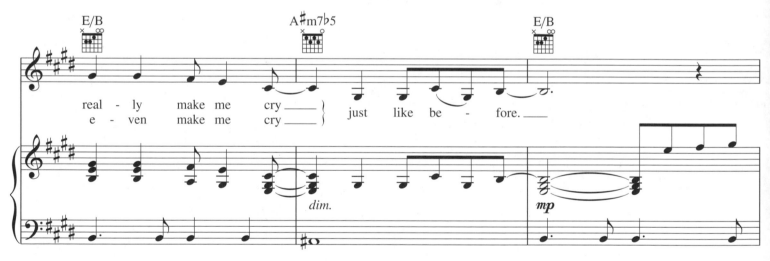

When they get to the part __ where he's break - in' her heart, _ it can

All my best mem - o - ries __ come back clear - ly to me; __ some can

real - ly make me cry _____ } just like be - fore. _

e - ven make me cry _____ }

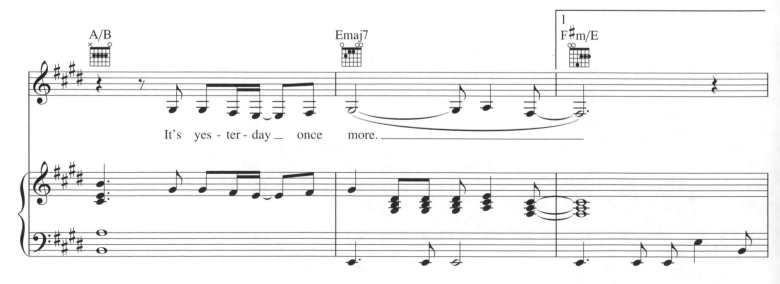

It's yes - ter - day _ once more. _____

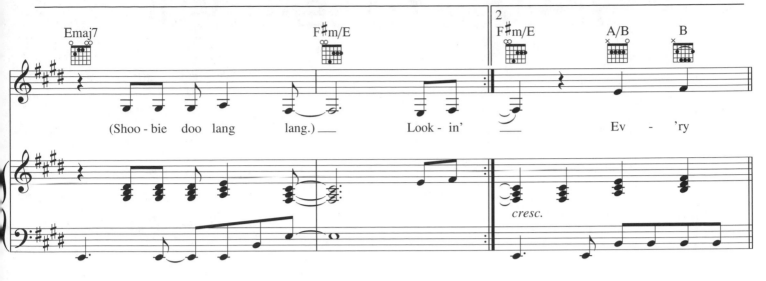

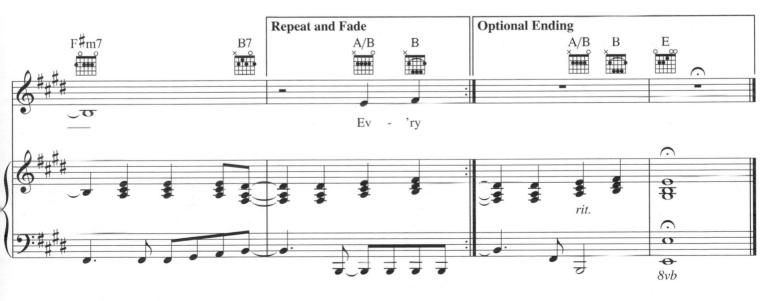

# YOU ARE SO BEAUTIFUL

Words and Music by BILLY PRESTON
and BRUCE FISHER

**Moderately slow, expressively**

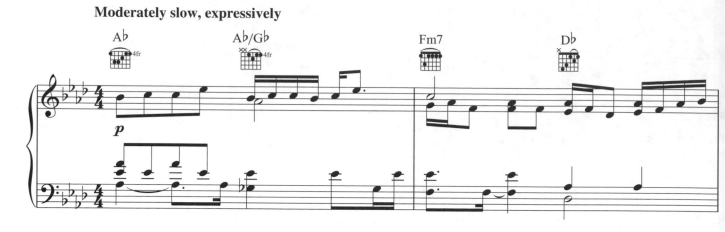

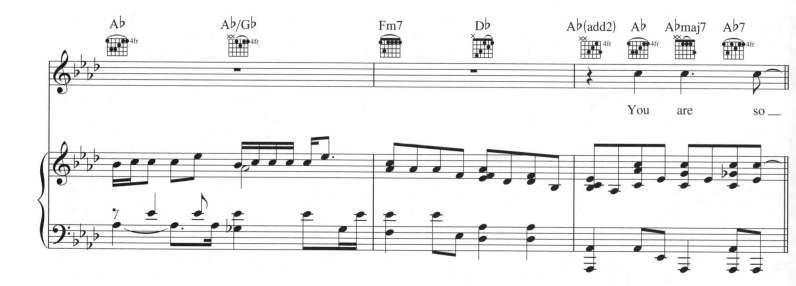

You are so ___

___ beau - ti - ful ___

to

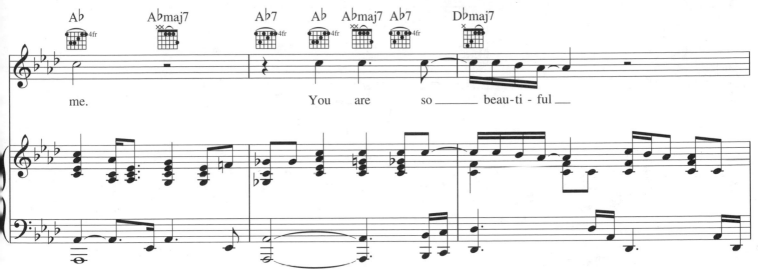

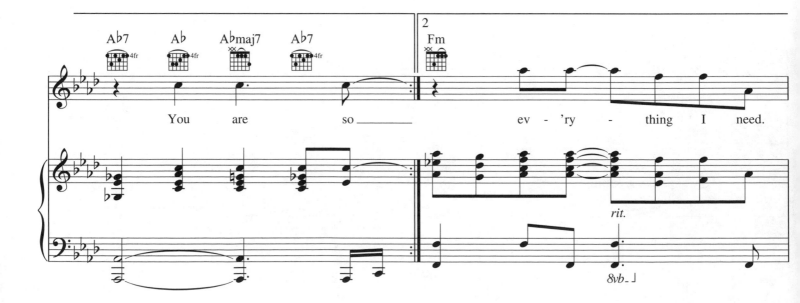

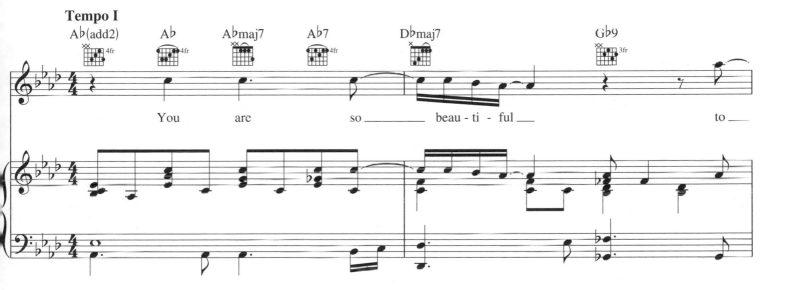

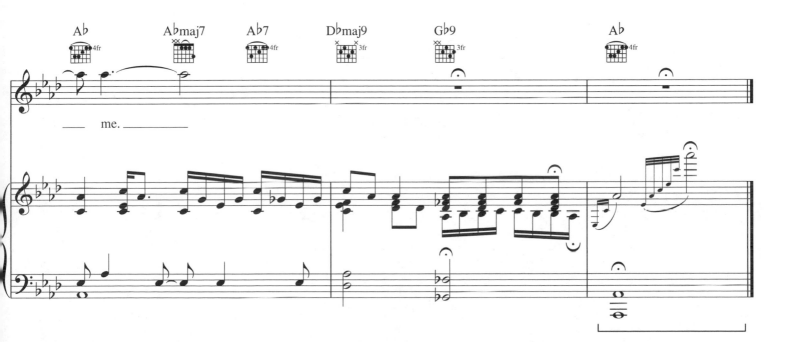

# YOU ARE THE SUNSHINE OF MY LIFE

Words and Music by
STEVIE WONDER

Moderately, with feeling

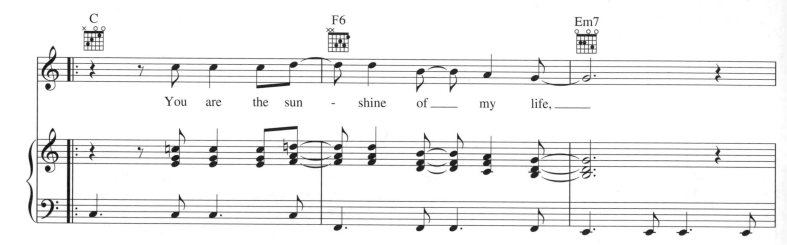

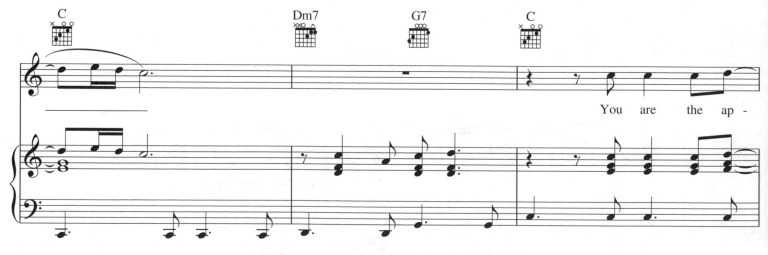

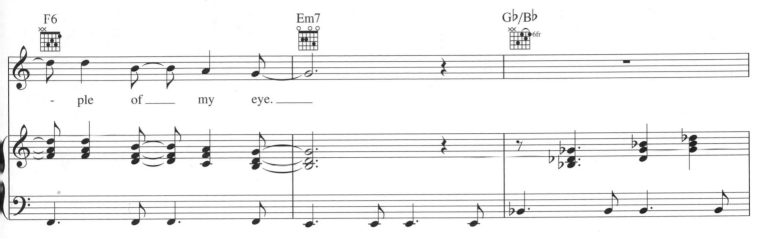

-ple of ___ my eye. ___

For - ev - er you'll ___ stay in ___ my heart, _____

I feel like this ___ is the ___ be -
You must have known ___ that I ___ was

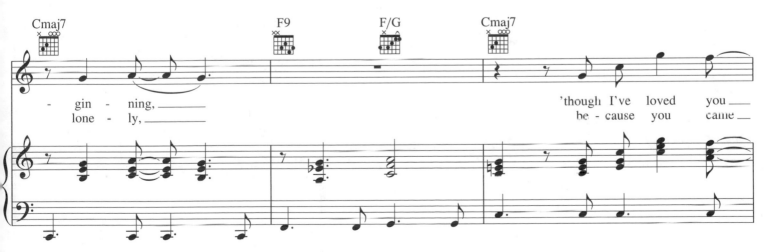

- gin - ning, _____
lone - ly, _____

'though I've loved you ___
be - cause you came ___

for a mil - lion years.
to my res - cue.

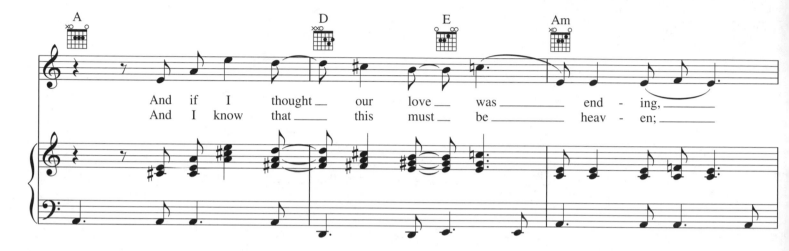

And if I thought our love was end - ing,
And I know that this must be heav - en;

I'd find my - self drown - ing in my own
how could so much love be in - side of

tears.
you?

Whoa, whoa.
Whoa.

# YOU'D BE SURPRISED

Words and Music by
IRVING BERLIN

**Moderately slow Bounce, with a lilt**

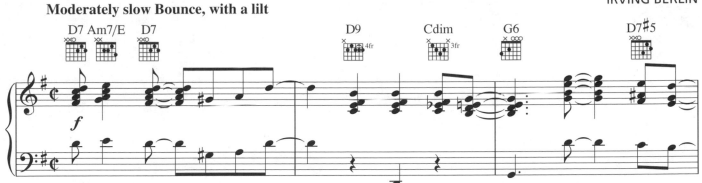

He's not so good in a crowd _ but when you get him a - lone, _
good in the house _ but on a bench in the park, _

you'd be sur - prised. _ He is - n't much at a dance _ but then when
you'd be sur - prised. _ He is - n't much in the light _ but when he

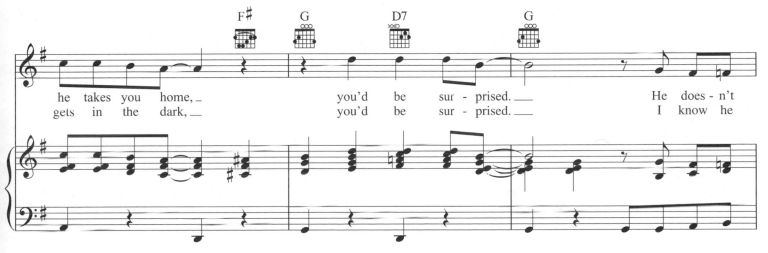

he takes you home, _ you'd be sur - prised. _ He does - n't
gets in the dark, _ you'd be sur - prised. _ I know he

look like much of a lov - er, _____ but don't judge a book __ by its cov -
looks as slow as the E - rie, _____ you don't know the half __ of it, dear -

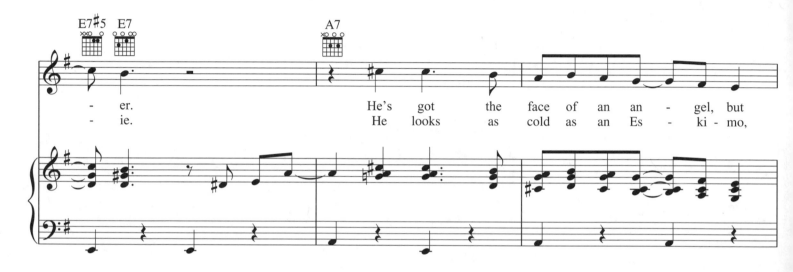

- er.
- ie.
He's got the face of an an - gel, but
He looks as cold as an Es - ki - mo,

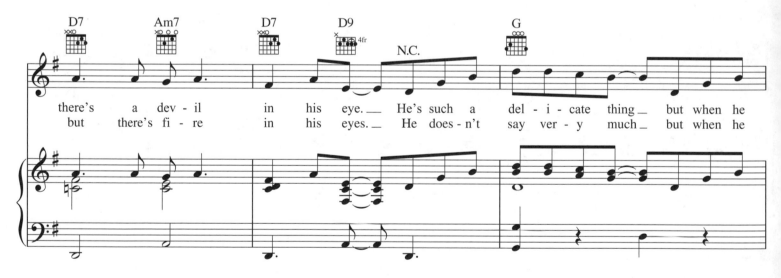

there's a dev - il in his eye. __ He's such a del - i - cate thing __ but when he
but there's fi - re in his eyes. __ He does - n't say ver - y much __ but when he

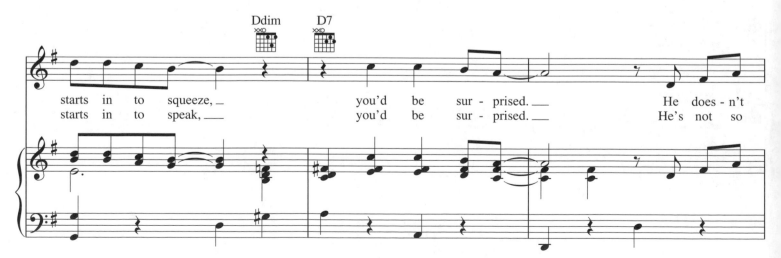

starts in to squeeze, __ you'd be sur - prised. __ He does - n't
starts in to speak, ___ you'd be sur - prised. __ He's not so

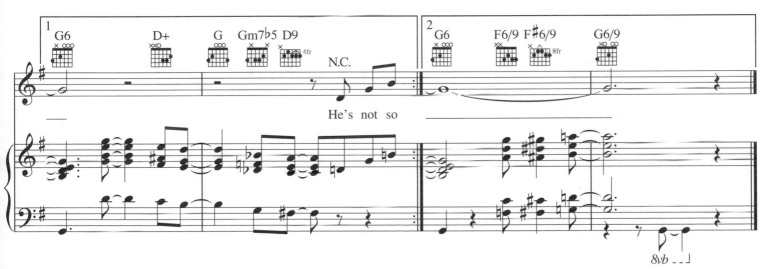

# YOU TOOK ADVANTAGE OF ME

## from PRESENT ARMS

Words by LORENZ HART
Music by RICHARD RODGERS

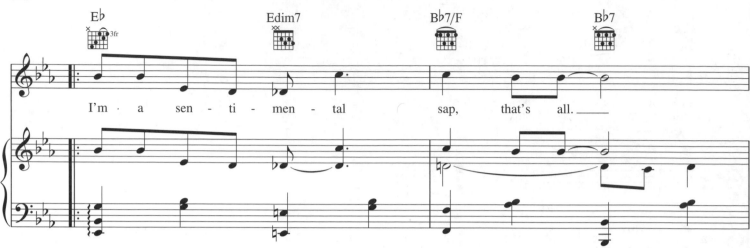

I'm a sen-ti-men-tal sap, that's all. ___

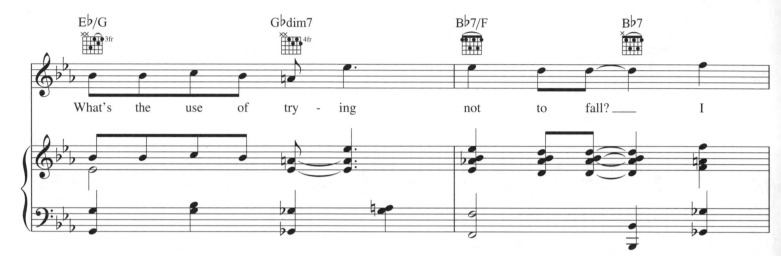

What's the use of try-ing not to fall? ___ I

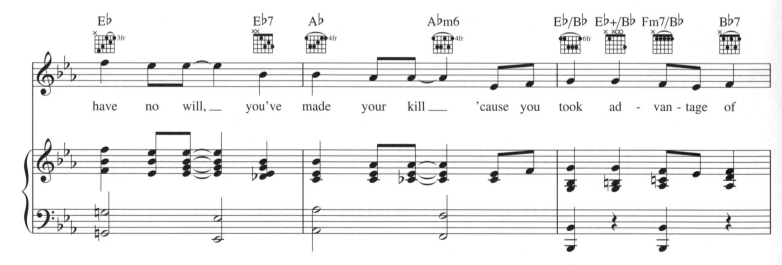

have no will, ___ you've made your kill ___ 'cause you took ad-van-tage of

me! I'm just like an ap-ple on a bough, ___

and you're gon-na shake me down some-how._ So what's the use,_ you've

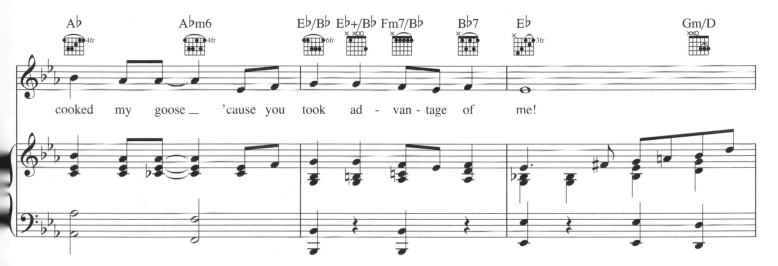

cooked my goose_ 'cause you took ad-van-tage of me!

I'm so hot and both-ered that I don't know_ my el-bow from_ my

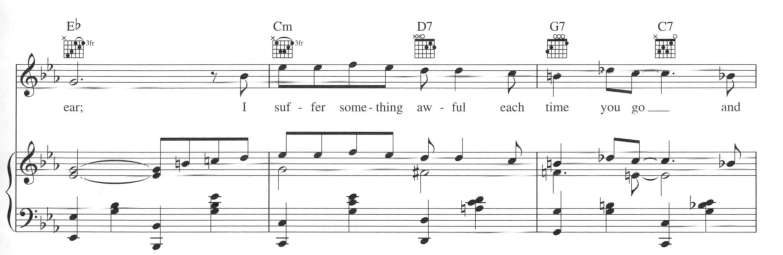

ear; I suf-fer some-thing aw-ful each time you go_ and

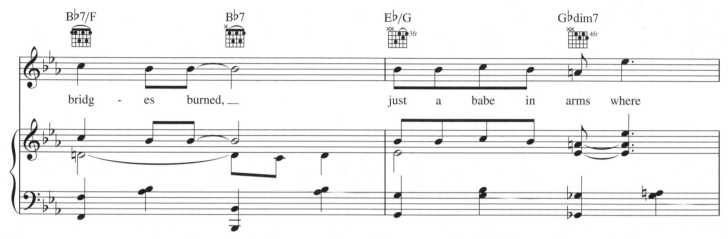

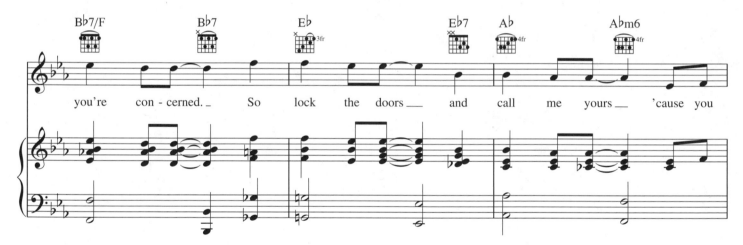

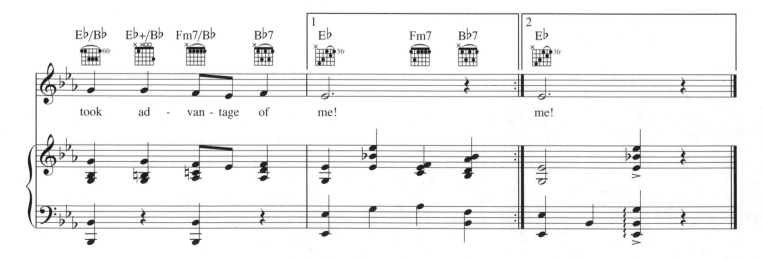